BUYING A HOUSE

A STEP BY STEP GUIDE BY

BY TERRY GORRY B.COMM, SOLICITOR

Visit http://BusinessAndLegal.ie (Terry Gorry & Co. Solicitors)

Copyright

All rights reserved. No part of this publication may be reproduced, distributed, or transmitted in any form or by any means, including photocopying, recording, or other electronic or mechanical methods, without the prior written permission of the publisher, except in the case of brief quotations embodied in critical reviews and certain other non-commercial uses permitted by copyright law.

For permission requests, contact the publisher at: Terry Gorry, Terry Gorry & Co. Solicitors, Enfield, Co. Meath, Ireland.

Text copyright © Terry Gorry

All Rights Reserved

1st August 2020, Enfield, County Meath

I first published this book in 2014, made some updates in 2016 and updated it again in July/August 2020 to include extra material including

-the Help to Buy grant for first time buyers,

-statements and representations made in the lead up to the signing of the contract of sale,

-deed of confirmation in respect of a gift received,

-tips for successful negotiations,

-closing day and what to expect and what you should do,

-and buying property for cash.

DISCLAIMER

Although the author and publisher have made every effort to ensure that the information in this book was correct at press time, the author and publisher do not assume and hereby disclaim any liability to any party for any loss, damage, or disruption caused by errors or omissions, whether such errors or omissions result from negligence, accident, or any other cause.

The material contained in this book is provided for general information purposes only and does not constitute legal or other professional advice. Whilst every care has been taken in the preparation of the content of all pages in this book, specific legal advice should always be sought on the application of the law in any particular situation.

We strongly recommend employing a legal professional to interpret and advice on ANY aspect of the law.

Table of Contents

COPYRIGHT 2

DISCLAIMER 4

INTRODUCTION 7

CHAPTER 1 GETTING STARTED AND FINDING THE RIGHT PROPERTY 9

CHAPTER 2 31

STATEMENTS AND REPRESENTATIONS MADE TO YOU 31

CHAPTER 3 MORTGAGES-FINANCING YOUR NEW PROPERTY 36

CHAPTER 4 FEES INVOLVED IN BUYING YOUR PROPERTY 50

CHAPTER 5 THE PHYSICAL PROPERTY, GETTING A STRUCTURAL SURVEY, AND PLANNING ISSUES 55

CHAPTER 6 CONVEYANCING-THE LEGAL STUFF 73

CHAPTER 7 BOOKING DEPOSITS AND CONTRACT DEPOSITS   96

CHAPTER 8 BUYING AN APARTMENT   100

CHAPTER 9 BUYING A NEW HOUSE OR APARTMENT VERSUS BUYING SECOND HAND   105

CHAPTER 10 BUYING IN IRELAND FROM ABROAD   111

CHAPTER 11 BONUS CHAPTER-SELLING YOUR HOUSE   115

ABOUT THE AUTHOR   125

Introduction

I'm almost certainly the only solicitor in Ireland with a teleporter licence.

A teleporter, in case you didn't know, is like a fork lift truck except it's bigger-much bigger-and the size of a tractor. It also has a telescopic boom which allows the forks to be extended out up to 20 metres, which is ideal, for example, for lifting up slates or tiles when roofing a 2/3 storey building.

That's what I needed it for in 2009.

I got my licence when I was building a block of 8 apartments in Edgeworthtstown, Longford.

Just before the property crash.

Let me explain: I have been involved in various businesses in Ireland since 1986, and all of them had a significant property development element to them.

The development in Edgeworthtstown was my first direct labour construction project. I bought the site, organised the direct labour, materials, and tradesmen-and drove the teleporter.

It was clear from early on that being able to drive the teleporter would save me hiring a driver, and quite a lot of money.

So, what has that to do with you buying a house or apartment?

I think it's fair to say that my experience as a solicitor, and as a builder/developer, makes me uniquely qualified to write this book to help you buy a good house. I don't believe there are too many people in Ireland who have seen "both sides of the fence" as closely as I have. You could say that I started right at the ground floor.

So, this book is a mixture of practical advice grounded in the legal realities of buying a residential property in Ireland, from someone who has walked in your footsteps-and who advises people, just like you, about property purchase and sales on a daily basis now. I have bought and sold property in Ireland since my first purchase at the tender age of 23: a commercial/residential property in Glasnevin, Dublin.

I have purchased and sold houses, apartments, shop units, green fields, sites, a petrol station, a pub, and actually carried out the development, by way of direct labour, in Longford where I learned to drive the teleporter.

By the end of this book, I believe you will have a clearer picture of what to look for, what to avoid, and enjoy/endure much reduced stress levels in buying your property.

You will know what is going on at every step of the way and what to expect next.

Chapter 1 Getting Started and Finding the Right Property

Before starting your property hunt, be crystal clear about what you can afford. It is understandable that you will be excited, particularly if it is your first property purchase.

But look closely at your finances, calculate the approximate monthly payments you will need to make, and make sure that you can afford them.

Also, do not leave yourself so tight financially that if you were sick, or laid off from your job for a few months, or met with some unforeseen circumstance, that you simply could not afford to pay your mortgage.

Leave yourself a little room to manoeuvre, a bit of wriggle room, and you will be not just able to afford your property a little easier, but you will also have a life.

Later, I take a close look at mortgages and other costs of buying your property. But for now, you need to decide whether to go with a mortgage broker or other intermediary or deal directly with the banks yourself. (I look at the advantages and disadvantages later too.)

Once you are approved, get an "offer in principle" from the lender. This will do two things:

1.-Give you peace of mind and

2.-give you an advantage over other interested parties because proof that you have loan approval will be of benefit in having your offer on a property accepted, because the auctioneer may be under instructions to obtain a quick sale, and a loan approved buyer will help him in this regard, and make him look good in the eyes of his client.

Once you have your letter of loan offer, you will know what you are able to spend.

Do not stray outside your limit and be ruthless with yourself when arranging viewings. It is extremely easy to get carried away when you start viewing properties and forget about your finances and budget.

It can also be easy to succumb to the sales patter of experienced auctioneers/property service providers, not to mention the clever, professional presentation of properties you are viewing.

Do not be fooled; stick with your game plan and do not let yourself fall in love with a property that does not fit your criteria.

When considering your finances, remember that you will also have other costs such as

1.-Stamp duty (see more in the finances chapter)

2.-Land registry fees & outlays

3.-Legal fee to your solicitor

4.-Structural survey report fee

5.-Valuation report fee.

Don't overlook these necessary outlays, as it is easy to just focus solely on the house price, and then leave yourself with a "hole" in your budget before you start repaying your mortgage.

How to spot a good property

The best way to find a good house is, paradoxically, to avoid a bad one. Decisions about schools for children, proximity to your workplace, good public transport are all factors which I am sure you will have considered closely.

But when you start viewing properties, what should you look out for?

Without having a survey carried out, there are some tell tale signs you need to look for:

a) Signs of damp-is there any signs of damp or a musty smell in the property?

If so, be careful because damp can be a serious problem that is hard to sort out, depending on the source of the damp. A property that is simply damp because it has not been occupied for some time is a different animal from one which as a problem with, for example, rising damp. And signs of rising damp should be investigated closely by your surveyor.

b) Look closely at the exterior of the house and see that the roof is not sagging, and the windows are level and not off plumb. You are simply looking to see that the house is horizontally and vertically correct.

Look also for signs of cracking in either the plasterwork or brickwork; some cracks are more serious than others. For example, cracks under windows may indicate structural instability or subsidence and would certainly warrant further investigation. The two big areas here are the roof and structural problems; putting these two areas right can be costly so avoiding a money pit at the outset is critical.

c) Has the property been properly looked after and has it received some TLC? Look for poor repair jobs or "patch up" repairs which may indicate an ambivalent attitude of the owners to carrying out proper and necessary repairs.

d) Look for expensive items that might need updating eg bathrooms, kitchens, windows, flooring can be expensive to upgrade or replace.

e) Check the services, specifically the electrics, plumbing, and the heating system (including the boiler) are up to date, and the boiler has been regularly serviced.

LOCATION, LOCATION, LOCATION

It's a well known truism when it comes to property that there are 3 critically important things to look out for:

1. Location

2. Location

3. Location.

Despite the unprecedented property crash in Ireland from 2008 onwards, despite the questioning of property as a good investment, despite a lot of things-one thing remains true. The location of your property is the single most important thing to look out for.

All you have to do is look at the significant improvement in property values in 2014/2015/16, and you will see that the first place to see recovery of prices, and the biggest and quickest recovery in prices, has been Dublin.

So, buy in the best location you can afford. You can change a lot of things about your property, and you can add value, build extensions, patios, decking etc.

But there is one thing you cannot change: the location of your property.

My advice? Buy the worst property in the best area, rather than the best property in the worst area.

Estate agents/auctioneers

The most likely source of your new property will be through an estate agent/auctioneer.

However, you may come across a "private sale" directly from the homeowner, who may be trying to save money by selling the property herself and avoid an auctioneer's fee. Buying and selling a house can be a fraught enough experience, to be frank, because there is a lot of stress, and emotions, involved in buying or selling a property.

Dealing directly with the vendor, in the absence of a professional mediator such as an auctioneer, can be problematic as the vendor will have a significant emotional investment in the property, and if you try to negotiate by pointing out shortcomings of the property you can find the vendor taking your comments "personally" and the relationship quickly sliding downhill.

REPOSSESSED PROPERTIES

You may also come across a bank repossession property, but the likelihood is that this property will be sold through an estate agent.

There are a few aspects of buying a repossessed property which are different from a property which is occupied by its owners; the principal one is that the contract, which will be drafted by the vendor's (bank's) solicitor, will be quite tightly drafted, and will be very much on a "take it or leave it" basis.

You may well be getting a bargain from a price viewpoint, but the tradeoff is a contract which favours the vendor to a greater extent than normal. This is not a huge problem, quite frankly, but is something that needs to be considered.

This would not be the case with buying a "normal" house, as there would be a certain amount of negotiation of the conditions of the contract between the solicitors acting for vendor and purchaser.

One of the main features of repossessed properties will be that they will not have received the same care and attention shown to them as occupied, lived in properties, and are almost certainly not going to be in great condition.

Let's face it: if your house was going to be repossessed, you would not be too motivated to carry out necessary repairs, or renovations, or lavish too much care and attention on it.

Buying new/off plan

Buying a new property off plan was not a feature in the Irish property market to any extent since the crash of 2008-2010. However, the succeeding years has seen a return to a steady, albeit lower level, supply of new properties. I take a look at buying new later in this book.

Buying at auction

Buying at auction is different from buying by "private treaty", which is the typical method of purchase through an auctioneer.

The big difference is when you buy at auction you sign the contract there and then and pay over 10% of the contract price. You are now bound to complete the purchase, even if you discover problems with the property later on, or even if other problems arise-for example, being unable to raise the necessary finance.

So, it is absolutely critical that you have your due diligence carried out <u>before</u> going to the auction at all, and that you have finance arranged.

Before going to an auction, you should ensure three things:

1. have your solicitor check out the legalities of the deal including the contract, and the title to the property, and

2. have an engineer or architect survey the property to check its structural soundness and

3. ensure you have your finances arranged.

Do not buy unless you have these three conditions fulfilled.

Buying at auction is also tremendously exciting, but it is easy to get carried away, so it's imperative that you go with a very fixed maximum price in your mind. And to ensure you do not get carried away, bring a friend or relation and tell them your limit, and ask them to remind you not to exceed it should the temperature in the auction room rise.

This happened me as a young man when I was after a property in Blackrock, County Dublin. I went along to the auction and got involved in a bidding war with one other individual. I completely blew my limit for the property out of the water but was outbid, thankfully. About three years later, I bought the same property for a considerably smaller sum.

I have also acted for the vendor in selling properties at an Allsops auction in 2014 and have taken calls from purchaser's solicitors after the event who had only just been approached by their client. At that stage, it is too late if there is a problem with the property as the contract has been signed and the purchaser had every opportunity, prior to attending the auction, to carry out his research referred to above.

The other solicitor had some queries about the contract, which I helped her with. But the bottom line was: there wasn't a thing in the world she could do about it because the contract was available for inspection before the auction and her client had gone ahead, signed the contract and bought the property.

Quite frankly, it is too late to discover problems after the auction and you have signed a contract.

Fixer Uppers

A fixer upper is a property that requires a good deal of attention and, more often than not, money. Unless you are an experienced fixer upper or small builder or have done this type of thing before, be careful. A "little gem" of a house that just needs a little "tender loving care" can soon become a money pit if you do not know what you are doing.

Whether you should take on such a property will depend on many things including how much time you will have on your hands, whether you need to live in the house when work is being done, whether you have small children, your diy skills, your budget, what work needs to be done, how much you can do yourself, and other factors.

Just be careful, and do your due diligence before you consider buying the properly at all because an attractive diy project can turn into a monster of a renovation with no end-in terms of money or time- in sight.

Always get an experienced surveyor/architect/engineer with professional indemnity insurance to carry out an inspection before investing your money. Even if you are determined to go ahead the property survey can be a good negotiating tool to have the price reduced.

BUYING PROPERTY WITH A FRIEND

Buying property with a friend can be problematic, and you need to do so with your eyes wide open. You need to consider:

-what happens if one of you loses your job or decides to emigrate or goes and gets married or finds a "new best friend" or spouse/partner?

-obtain good legal advice and have a shared ownership agreement drawn up. Do keep in mind that this agreement will be between you and your friend, and the bank is not a party to it, but your agreement should deal with what happens if one of you want to move on, if one of you loses your job, if you pay extra contributions or a bigger deposit, etc.

-as stated above, the lender will not be a party to the shared ownership agreement, so each of you will still be jointly and severally liable in full for the mortgage, regardless of what you may have agreed in the agreement.

DEALING WITH THE AUCTIONEER

Once you have found a property you are interested in, you will need to contact the auctioneer to arrange a viewing.

Be very clear that the auctioneer's job is to sell the property for his client, the owner of the house. So, he will paint the property in the best possible light, and in doing so, may well make some statements that are not entirely true.

Quite frankly, he may "overegg the pudding". He may make statements which could generously be described as exaggerations or flights of fancy, but you must be very grounded, and take what is said with a certain degree of skepticism.

If an auctioneer makes a material misrepresentation to you, you may have a case for negligent misstatement against him. But, trust me on this: you really don't want to be in that situation. So, to avoid it, be skeptical.

And one thing you must understand is this: if you buy the property, once the contract is issued it will almost certainly contain a special condition stating that you cannot rely on any representations made by the auctioneer. So, that may shut off the avenue of any legal action for negligent misstatement, should the need arise.

Hopefully, you will not find yourself in this situation.

The bottom line is you should take what the auctioneer says with a giant grain of salt.

Make sure you fully carry out your own enquiries and do not rely blindly on what the auctioneer says.

Trust, but verify.

Negotiating price

If you want to ensure the lowest possible price for your house, do not let the auctioneer know at the outset what your budget is.

Instead, "low ball" him, so that if your budget is €200,000, tell him your budget is €175,000.

He will probably show you houses with prices in excess of €175,000 anyway, but when he does, you will be in a slightly stronger position to negotiate because you have already told him your budget is €175,000.

He will recognise that there is a pretty tight limit to how much above this he can negotiate out of you, but you can still be within your budget and comfort zone.

If you are in a hurry, don't tell him this because it will be fed back to the sellers who will then assume they are in a stronger position than you, and may think they can pressurise you into a quick purchase.

Do let the agent know that you are finance approved or a cash buyer, assuming this is the case, and that you are happy to proceed quickly but that your prime priorities are value for money and coming in under budget.

When viewing the property, put on your best poker face; even if you love the place, don't take out a measuring tape and start measuring for new curtains or discussing with your partner the changes you are going to make or where you are going to put your best furniture.

The estate agent, if he is any good, will be watching your face like a hawk for tell tale signs and your reactions generally. If he is a good auctioneer he will be able to get an accurate handle on your opinion of the property.

But don't feed it to him on a plate.

Instead of betraying your true feelings, ask some questions-for example, why is the house being sold, how many people have viewed it, how many have been back for a 2nd viewing, etc-all the while maintaining your cool, calm, and collected look. Let the agent know that you are looking at other properties too, and let him know how many imminent viewings you have arranged.

In fact, when you are making your appointment to view let him know that you are pretty busy looking at houses.

Make sure that you have your research done before making any offer, the most important of which is what similar properties in the area have sold for, whether the market is rising or falling, and so on.

When you are making your offer, remember this: you cannot insult an auctioneer!

So, don't be afraid to offer below the asking price-how much below is a judgment call. And when you are making your offer, don't be afraid to compare it to other houses you have seen and let him know that this offer is the best you can do because you are going to have to spend money on various parts of the house.

And don't be afraid to spell out the areas you feel will require investment, even if it is work you can put off for a few years.

Once you have made your offer, the estate agent is obliged to put it to his client.

But listen closely to what the auctioneer says because you can read a lot from the reaction. A complete and outright rejection of your offer because it is one which the clients are not going to accept, compared to one which indicates that he thinks this offer is too low are two qualitatively different responses.

The latter response is simply asking for another offer, you might not be a million miles away, and it is not being rejected out of hand.

The agent will come back to you with his client's response and you will be invited to make another, improved offer.

This again is a judgment call but make sure to stay within your budget, and don't be afraid to play hardball and tell the odd little white lie. If you are going to make another offer, don't make it there and then; sleep on it and let the auctioneer sweat a little.

All is fair in love, war, and property negotiations.

Negotiating tips

Negotiating.

Haggling.

Some people, like my mother, love negotiating, and have done so all their life.

Some people, like my wife, hate haggling. I think people like this feel it is insulting to the other party. But often, the other party expects you to haggle or negotiate, and are ready for it. In fact, they have probably built the negotiation into their price to begin with.

Being able to negotiate effectively is a vital skill, one which can serve you in all walks of life-from your career to buying a car to buying other goods to buying property to negotiating in relationships/family etc.

As a solicitor, I have to negotiate often on behalf of clients, and I have made it my business to study the top negotiators to do the best job I can as well as drawing on my own experience in negotiating property deals since 1986.

The Most Important Negotiation Tactic-Detachment

The single most important tip is not to care too much. If you do, and you make it blatantly obvious that you very badly want this car/house/suit/holiday, you weaken your negotiating position from the outset.

Because the other party knows how badly you want it. What you need to do is maintain an air of detachment-sure, you want the thing, but not that badly. You are ready to walk away if the deal is not right.

As soon as the other party things, "Jeez, this guy is going to walk away, he must have other options", you are in a far stronger position.

And giving this impression is entirely within your control.

So, care, alright, but not too much.

Also, if and when you are walking away because the gap between you is too large, and the other party offers you his business card "in case you change your mind", don't take it. Reverse the balance of power by giving him your business card or contact details, and tell him, "give me a call if you change your mind".

Remember, you don't have to buy this car at this garage, you can buy a different car or not buy one at all. But you have the money, and he needs the sale.

There are two ways to ensure you don't care too much:

Get someone else to negotiate for you

Recognise the difference between loving and liking-think about how you will feel in 20 years' time about this thing you are trying to acquire. This will allow you to become more detached.

Maximize the Other Party's Investment/Commitment

If you can get the other party to invest a lot of time in trying to win you over it puts you in a stronger position. Why?

Because they have already invested quite a lot in you. And we know that the more a person has invested in something the more desirable it becomes for them.

Let's say you are buying a motor car, or indeed anything in retail, and you spend a lot of time at the car dealers, but don't buy. The car salesman has invested quite a lot in you yet has got no return whatsoever.

Then you go back another day, and spend even more time discussing the potential deal. The more time the car salesman spends on you the more reluctant he will be to see you walk off and go to another dealer. He is far more likely to cave after spending all this time, especially if he knows he has competition.

You will, of course, have told him you are looking at other cars in the competitor garage.

Start Friendly and Cooperative with an Air of Incompetence

If you start friendly and cooperative you can always get more aggressive and adopt a "tough guy" stance later.

But if you start with the "tough guy" stance you will have no credibility later on when you try to be nice and friendly, and claim you misspoke.

If the other party starts aggressive, let them.

Take it, take notes because inside they are thinking "this is going to be easy" when, in fact, all they are doing is investing more time in you. Ultimately, this will make it harder for them to walk. They will be like someone investing a load of money into a slot machine and being encouraged to try another machine.

No way will they walk, because they have put too much into this machine and it must be due to payout.

You want to be more like the private investigator Columbo than Confucius, the Chinese teacher and philosopher.

If you appear to be incompetent, or inexperienced and say to the other party, "look, I'm new to this, you are extremely experienced and have been around a long time, maybe you could help me here" there is a good chance they will respond well to this approach.

Deadlines are Important but Negotiable

The vast majority of concessions and deals are done towards the end, near the deadline. Don't be afraid to exploit this fact.

For example, you spend a good bit of time negotiating the purchase of an expensive piece of clothing. Just when the vendor is happy he has you on the hook, and you are now due to pull out the credit card, you say, "can't you throw in a couple of ties?" You will have a great chance of getting the ties, or a few pairs of socks, or whatever is appropriate.

But deadlines are the product of negotiations, therefore are negotiable. However, the passing of a deadline can actually be the opening up of an opportunity.

How?

Ask, as they are quitting, "where did I go wrong?". They will say, "when it's over, we'll tell you".

And another deadline can be negotiated. Things are never over while relationships continue.

How many times have we seen political deadlines slip in the North of Ireland, for example, but eventually agreement is reached? It's never over until it's over.

BOOKING DEPOSIT

If your offer is accepted, you will have to pay a booking deposit.

The booking deposit is fully refundable-that is, if the sale does not go ahead or you change your mind or for whatever reason the sale falls through, it should be returned to you with no questions asked. The auctioneer only holds this deposit as "stakeholder", and not as agent for the vendor.

This deposit, the booking deposit, is not to be confused with the contract deposit which I will deal with in the section dealing with the contract and legalities.

A typical booking deposit will range from €3000 to €10000, depending on the price of the house.

RENT OR BUY?

Are you fully committed to buying your house, or is there a niggling doubt in the back of your mind as to whether you should continue renting?

Remember that the debate of buy versus rent only arises if you look at your home from an investment point of view. Clearly, if you decide that you simply want to buy a property, live in it, and eventually hand it on to your child(ren), then the academic debate as to the best financial approach between renting and buying does not arise.

But if you are in two minds, or if you are not sure, there are a number of things to consider.

Firstly, you can find any number of "rent v buy" calculators online which compares the cost of renting versus buying over a good period of time. One useful one can be found on the MyHome.ie website at www.myhome.ie

This calculator looks at 3 scenarios and what the position would be in year 10:

1. If you buy an apartment for, say €220,000, after 10 years you will still owe €166,055 and will have paid €126, 306 so the 10 year cost is €292,361

2. If you rent for 5 years and then buy, you will owe €182,511 and will have paid €168,860 between rent and mortgage payments so the total cost at year 10 will be €351,371

3. If you rent for 10 years and then purchase, you will have incurred a cost of €142,440 and still owe €192,015 giving you a total cost of €334,455 at year 10.

So, the answer in this scenario assuming an interest rate of 6% over 30 years and savings rate average of 3.2% is to buy now.

Many of these calculators need to be taken with a grain of salt because the assumptions underlying their creation about interest rates, property value changes, rental values, taxation, etc. could have serious impacts on the outcomes.

PROS AND CONS OF RENTING VERSUS BUYING

-Renting gives you greater flexibility and potential mobility, especially if you are still in the early stages of your career or family life

-Interest rates can accumulate significantly over a period of 30 years ensuring that the actual amount you pay for a house with a purchase price of €140,000 will be €235,000

-One month's rent as a deposit is sufficient when renting whereas the new central bank guidelines in relation to minimum deposit requirements ensure that you will have a serious amount of saving and scrimping to do to meet the criteria for a mortgage

-Renting means you don't have to worry about local property tax or stamp duty

-You don't have to worry about negative equity or a massive outstanding mortgage which appears to be of Himalayan proportions in the early years

-Buying may turn out to be a great investment, though, over the course of the mortgage so not only do you have a place to live in and call your own, but you may significantly grow your capital

-Paying a mortgage on your own behalf is not dead money, unlike paying rent which ensures that you are paying off your landlord's mortgage

USING THE INTERNET TO RESEARCH

The internet is an incredibly powerful tool to help you with your property search.

For starters, you can view a huge amount of properties on sites like Daft.ie and auctioneers' websites, and save you a huge amount of time ringing around looking at properties.

You can also find out what properties have sold for on sites like MyHome.ie.

This site, and others, pulls in data from the Residential Property Price Register which is produced by the Property Services Regulatory Authority (PSRA) pursuant to section 86 of the Property Services (Regulation) Act 2011. It includes Date of Sale, Price and Address of all residential properties purchased in Ireland since the 1st January 2010, as declared to the Revenue Commissioners for stamp duty purposes and can be found at this web address. https://www.propertypriceregister.ie/website/npsra/pprweb.nsf/PPR?OpenForm

This website also maintains a register of registered property service providers, in case you are dealing with an estate agent that you are concerned about.

You can even use Google maps and street view to have a virtual snoop around the area of your target property.

So, don't be afraid to use all the tools at your disposal to ensure that you get the best property for you.

Chapter 2

Statements and representations made to you

You need to be cautious and vigilant about the statements you are tempted to rely on, and who is making those statements.

Let me explain.

I act for large numbers of people who are buying (or selling) property. When I meet the purchasers or speak to them on the phone they frequently tell me "the auctioneer said" or "the developer said" or "the seller said".

I have to tell them to ignore, or at the very least treat with a great deal of caution, these statements because from a legal perspective they cannot rely on them. Because invariably when the auctioneer's sales advice note issues or when the contract is issued by the vendor's solicitor there will be disclaimers and conditions along the lines that the purchaser cannot rely on any statement outside of the written contract of sale.

And that the contract contains the entire agreement between the purchaser and vendor.

In other words, the vendor's solicitor will go to the trouble in many cases of inserting a special condition similar to the following:

Entire Agreement and Representations

The purchasers agree and accept that no statement or measurement contained in any brochure or advertisement issued by the Vendor or any agent on behalf of the Vendor relating to the Subject Property shall constitute a representation inducing the Purchasers to enter into the sale or any warranty forming part of this Agreement.

Any statement, description or measurement contained in in any such particulars or in any verbal form given by or on behalf of the Vendor is for illustrative purposes and are not to be given as matters of fact.

Any misstatement or omission or mis-description or incorrect information given verbally or in form of any printed particulars by any person on the Vendor's behalf shall not give rise to any cause of action claim or compensation or to any right of rescission under this Agreement.

The Purchaser shall have no right of action against any agent, employee or any person whatsoever connected directly or indirectly with the Vendor whereby any mistake, omission, discrepancy, innaccuracy, misstatement or misrepresentation may have been published or communicated to the Purchaser during the course of any representation or negotiation leading up to the sale.

This Agreement constitutes the entire agreement between the parties hereto with respect to the subject matter hereof and supersedes and extinguishes any representations or warranties (if any) previously given or made accepting those contained in the Agreement and no variation shall be effective unless agreed and signed by the parties or by some person duly authorised by each of them.

You will also note that the sales advice note from the auctioneer/estate agent will be "subject to contract/without prejudice/contract denied" which is an indication that you will only be able to rely on what is contained in the contract or is clarified/confirmed between the solicitors as they negotiate a binding contract.

It can be a struggle for the solicitor to temper the enthusiasm of the inexperienced purchaser because they will assume what is being said to them by the agreeable vendor or estate agent can be relied on. Maybe it can, maybe it cannot and if there is a dispute you will need to look to the written agreement between the parties to see exactly where you stand.

And the written agreement between the parties is the Law Society Standard Conditions of Sale 2019 edition.

IDENTITY

11. (a) The Purchaser Accepts the evidence of identity as may be gathered from the documents specified in the Documents Schedule. The Vendor confirms that he has furnished to the Purchaser such information as is in his possession relative to the identity and extent of the Subject Property, but the Vendor is not and shall not be required to define exact boundaries, fences, ditches, hedges or walls or to specify which (if any) of the same are of a party nature, and the Vendor is not and shall not be required to identify parts of

the Subject Property held under different titles.

RIGHTS – LIABILITIES – CONDITION OF SUBJECT PROPERTY

13. The Vendor confirms that he has disclosed before the Date of Sale, in the Particulars the Special Conditions or otherwise, all easements, rights, reservations, exceptions, privileges, covenants, conditions, restrictions, rents, taxes and other liabilities (not already known to the Purchaser or apparent from inspection) which are known by the Vendor to affect the Subject Property and are likely to affect it following Completion.

14. Subject to General Condition 13, the Purchaser Accepts that the Subject Property is sold and the Purchaser shall be deemed to buy:

(a) with full notice of the actual state and condition of the Subject Property and

(b) subject to (i) all Leases (if any) mentioned in the Particulars or in the Special Conditions and (ii) all easements, rights, reservations, exceptions, privileges, covenants, conditions, restrictions, rents, taxes, liabilities, outgoings and all incidents of tenure affecting the Subject Property (each a "Relevant Provision") and

(c) notwithstanding any partial statement or description of the Lease or the Relevant Provision in the Particulars or in the Special Conditions or in any document specified in the Documents Schedule.

Conclusion

I hope you see from these conditions in the contract for the sale of property are sufficient to cast aside any warranty or representation that was made in the run up to the binding contract coming into effect.

And that you simply cannot rely on these statements, no matter how well intentioned or helpful or clarifying they were intended to be.

Chapter 3 Mortgages-Financing Your New Property

The first thing to consider when looking for a mortgage is affordability-be clear on what you can, and cannot afford. And remember interest rates can rise significantly over the course or your mortgage, and your own circumstances can also change.

So, make sure to "stress test" your mortgage to ensure you can continue paying it through rocky periods. An easy way to do this is to use an online mortgage calculator and play around with it using different, increasing rates of interest to see what your repayments will be.

SECURE INCOME?

Is your income secure? Lenders in Ireland have been badly burned in the last 15 years or so, and they now take a fairly cautious, prudent approach to lending.

You will also need to demonstrate a good savings track record with regular savings, low debt, regular monthly credit card payments, and no missed payments or poor record at the Irish Credit Bureau.

The Irish Credit Bureau is funded by the main lenders in Ireland and records, and shares, information about borrowers missed or non payments of loans.

How much can you borrow?

New mortgage lending guidelines were issued by the Central Bank of Ireland in January, 2015. At that time the position was as follows:

Central Bank Regulations

In summary, the maximum borrowing level is 3.5 times your gross income.

<u>Non first time buyer</u>: If you are not a first time buyer, you will need a deposit of 20% of the purchase price.

<u>First time buyer</u>: if you are a first time buyer, you will need a 10% deposit for houses up to €220,000. If the price of the house is over €220,000, you will need 10% of the first €220,000 and 20% for the amount over €220,000.

Investors will require a 30% deposit.

The key thing that lenders will look at when looking at your loan application is your ability to service the loan-that is, will the bank get their money back?

To ascertain this, they will look at your savings record, credit history, the sector/industry you are employed in, evidence gathered over a period of time that you can repay, even if interest rates were to rise by 2%.

Your income will also be closely scrutinized, especially the prospect of it increasing over time. Important factors here will be overtime, bonuses, and commission, and lenders now are reluctant to attribute too much importance to all of these elements unless they are satisfied that they will be recurring.

A critical factor is how safe your employment is, and a public servant such as a teacher, Garda, or nurse will be in a strong position here.

Self employed people on the other hand have a bit more persuading and selling to do, and will need to produce up to date accounts, and other evidence such as client lists, etc.

The Central Bank regulations governing limits on house loans were reviewed twice in 2017 and new rules came into effect in 2018. The key thing you need to understand is that the limits are concerned with loan to income and loan to value limits. For the most up to date limits when you are seeking to arrange finance head over to the Central Bank website at **centralbank.ie**.

Help to buy

A first time buyer who buys or builds between July 2016 and 31st December 2021 may be entitled to claim a refund of income tax and DIRT paid over the previous 4 years.

You must take out a mortgage of at least 70% of the purchase price (loan to value ratio) and the property must cost less than

€500,000. You must occupy the house for at least 5 years after it is habitable.

The amount of relief to which you may be entitled is up to 5% of the purchase price in respect of a house costing up to €400,000 with a maximum relief of €20,000. For a house costing between €400,000 and €500,000 the maximum relief is €20,000.

The application process is online and involves 2 stages: the application stage and claim stage. You make your claim through the Revenue Commissioner's website at Ros.ie through the Revenue's myAccount service or at ROS (Revenue Online Service) for self-assessed taxpayers.

DEAL DIRECTLY WITH LENDER OR USE A BROKER?

You will need to decide whether you are going to deal directly with the lender yourself, or use a mortgage broker/company who will have arrangements with a number of lenders. Using a broker/intermediary will have a cost attached, generally as a % of the loan advanced, but should save you a lot of time and allow your proposal to be submitted to a wide range of lenders.

On the other hand, if you are prepared to do the legwork yourself and are a pretty organized person, there is no reason why you cannot deal with the lenders yourself, and save yourself a commission to the broker.

A good, professional broker/intermediary should be of greater benefit than just a time saver; he should be able to give you sound advice, know the market well, which lenders have the most competitive products at any point in time, and so on.

So, it is a judgment call for yourself as to whether to use a broker or not. Just make sure that they are regulated by the Central Bank and ask to see their licence or other proof of registration.

Do watch out for incentives and gimmicks from lenders that may well be built into the price of your mortgage, or which will disappear and be of no benefit once you sign on the dotted line.

Just like a puppy, a mortgage is for life!

TYPES OF MORTGAGE

Mortgages can be divided into 2 broad categories: an annuity mortgage and an interest only mortgage.

The key elements of your mortgage will be the term and the interest rate. The longer your term, the lower the repayments will be but the more interest you will pay over the life of the mortgage.

A key decision for you will be whether to fix your interest rate or go with a variable rate.

The fixed rate will give you a huge degree of certainty and you will know exactly what you have to pay over the fixed rate period, which can range from 1 to 10 years.

However, if rates drop you will probably feel disgusted paying "over the odds" for your mortgage. And bear in mind that the advantage of the certainty you obtain at the outset with a fixed rate product will be reflected in the interest rate charged.

The variable rate will vary in accordance with the cost of funds to the bank from its sources. However, even if the Euribor (the European interbank ordinary rate) rate-the rate at which the banks borrow their money- is constant, there is no guarantee that banks will not put in some "sneaky" rate increases, and there is always criticism that banks do not pass on quickly enough, or all falls in Euribor interest rates.

Mortgages and Charges-the Legal Position

Mortgages and charges, and the different types of mortgages and charges can be confusing for many home-owners. A common question asked is, "what is the difference between a mortgage and a charge?"

There is a significant legal difference between a mortgage of a registered property and an unregistered property (the latter is registered in the registry of deeds, the former is registered in the Land Registry).

The difference in reality is that a registered property is 'charged' i.e. a charge is registered on the property at Land Registry but no formal transfer of ownership takes place.

An unregistered property is actually conveyed, assigned or leased by the borrower to the lending institution, subject to the borrower's right to redeem(pay off) the loan in the property. But title formally passes to the lending institution under the mortgage deed.

Approximately 90% of the land in Ireland is registered which represents 85% of titles. The title shown on a land registry folio is guaranteed by the state, so this gives you a great degree of comfort when buying registered property.

From a practical perspective as someone who is buying a property with a loan from the bank, there is no real difference to you.

THE MORTGAGE DEED

This document states that the lender has made a loan available to the borrower and the borrower guarantees to repay the loan by securing the loan against the property.

The mortgage deed will also contain a number of other covenants including

* A covenant to the effect that the property must be used as the borrower's principal private residence

* A covenant to not carry out any development on the property without the consent in writing of the lender

* A covenant to insure the property and have the interest of the lender noted on the policy.

It is important to bear in mind that these are standard covenants in mortgages with the main banks; it is crucial to read closely, or have a legal professional read, the additional covenants if dealing with a sub-prime lender or a smaller financial institution.

It is also important to note that the mortgage document will often refer back to the letter of loan offer which may contain additional covenants and conditions. It may also contain additional information about the circumstances relating to what will happen in the event of default in mortgage payments.

TYPES OF MORTGAGE

1. Principal Sums

This mortgage is for a fixed sum; it is less used in practice now as most banks will generally issue 'all sums due' mortgages.

2. All sums due

There is generally an "all sums due" clause in most mortgages now, and this has the potential to have a significant impact on your finances if you are unaware of what it means.

It means that the borrower is pledging their property as security not just for the loan to purchase the property in question, but for ALL indebtedness to the bank, now or in the future (credit card, car loan etc).

This is obviously of huge importance as many people will spread their financial exposure between various banks in an attempt to create a fence between different loans, but this clause means the bank can use the mortgaged property as security for all borrowing due to it.

THE CONTRACT OF SALE AND YOUR MORTGAGE

When you are buying a property your solicitor may insert a special condition making the purchase subject to loan approval. However, this became much less common as the market took off a few years ago, and the vendor's solicitor was reluctant to agree to this.

However, things have gone full circle now and in 2016 it is a recommendation/practice direction of the Law Society of Ireland that such clauses should be inserted in all contracts of sale, even where finance has been secured by the purchaser.

The drafting of this clause, if it is necessary and you do not have finance arranged, is important as it needs to cover circumstances where you eventually receive a loan offer but you are unable to comply with some of the conditions of the loan offer.

It should also provide for either party rescinding the contract should loan approval not be forthcoming.

Here is the Law Society recommended wording to be inserted in the contract:

This contract shall be subject to the purchaser obtaining approval for a loan of €xxxxxxx from [xxxxxxxxxx] on the security of the premises, provided always that if this loan has not been approved in writing within four weeks from the date hereof, either party shall be entitled to rescind this contract and in such event the purchaser shall be refunded his deposit without interest costs or compensation thereon.

If the loan approval is conditional on a survey satisfactory to the lending institution or a mortgage protection or a life insurance policy being taken out or the lending institution being satisfied at any time prior to drawdown of the loan that its valuation of the property has not changed since the date of loan approval or some other condition, compliance with which is not within the control of the purchaser, the loan shall not be deemed to be approved until the purchaser is in a position to accept and draw down the loan on terms which are within his reasonable power or procurement.

This clause will give you a good deal of protection if your finance, for whatever reason does not come through, or if the value of the property falls sufficiently to leave you short of funding to complete the sale.

YOUR SOLICITOR AND YOUR LENDER

In residential transactions, your solicitor is required to give an undertaking to the lender, together with proof of professional indemnity insurance, and eventually a "certificate of title" in an agreed format with the Law Society of Ireland.

This undertaking and certificate of title documentation is sent to your solicitor once your mortgage is approved.

The bank will only release the loan cheque to allow completion of the sale when they have received the solicitor's undertaking duly completed.

The undertaking obliges your solicitor to ensure

-that you will acquire good marketable title to the property

-that you have executed(signed) all the necessary loan documentation including mortgage deed etc.

-to register the mortgage in the appropriate registry (Registry of Deeds or Land Registry) as a legal charge on the property

-to lodge the title deeds and the solicitor's Certificate of Title with the lender once you have been registered as owner and the bank's charge registered on the property with the Property Registration Authority.

Circumstances may arise, for example if there is an unauthorised development on the property or an extension without planning permission or building regulations, where your solicitor will have to qualify the undertaking. Any such qualifications must be cleared in advance with the lender.

This undertaking by the solicitor is a profoundly serious matter for him, and if the fails to deliver on his undertaking, he can be reported to the Law Society, and sued on foot of it.

For this reason, a situation can develop where there is a problem with a document-for example a planning permission condition or a certificate of compliance with planning and building regulations-which you are happy to accept and proceed with the purchase, but your solicitor won't, because of his undertaking.

So, remember, even if you feel you are getting a real bargain and you're prepared to overlook some shortcoming in title or planning documentation, your solicitor's position and undertaking needs to be considered too, and he may not be able to proceed until the problem is properly resolved.

Self Build Houses and Stage Payment Mortgages

Perhaps you've decided to build a house yourself-either by direct labour or having it built by a building contractor? Many houses in Ireland in rural areas are built by direct labour in circumstances where a couple may have been given a site by parents or a family member.

If you are engaging the services of a building contractor, you will need a building contract/agreement.

This will cost in the region of €500 plus vat, but it may be the smartest investment you have ever made, because it will protect you in the event that there are problems or disputes with the builder as the build progresses.

Self-Build Mortgages

If you are lucky enough to be gifted a site from a parent or relative, or if you decide you want to build your house yourself you will probably finance the construction with a self-build mortgage. If the site is only going to be transferred to you, and not you and not your partner/spouse then he/she will have to get independent legal advice before signing the mortgage documents.

The bank will insist on this as your partner will be signing up for a mortgage on a property that he/she is not a registered owner of.

Self-build mortgages generally involve funds being released by your lender at various stages of the build, generally in six stages.

This ensures that you draw down funds only when you need them and avoid paying interest on the entire loan from day 1; as the build progresses you draw down the funds in tranches.

You will need to be in touch with your solicitor to facilitate each tranche payment who will have given an undertaking to the lending institution to only release funds provided the bank's criteria for release of funds are met. This will principally involve your engineer issuing a stage payment certificate.

This certificate will indicate to the lending institution what stage the build is at and the current value of the property to date. It will also confirm that the surveyor/supervising engineer has professional indemnity insurance.

Once your solicitor is in receipt of the stage payment certificate, he will then make the request to the lending institution for drawdown of the sum indicated by the engineer to bring the build to the next stage. The tranche of funds in question will be transferred to your solicitor who will pass it on to you to allow you pay your builder or individual sub-contractors.

Planning Search

Regardless of whether you are building by direct labour, or using a building contractor, you should carry out a planning search in the local planning office before commencing construction, or before signing a contract for purchase.

Alternatively, you can have a search carried out by professional law searchers.

Things to look out for include

-The zoning of your site

-The zoning of the adjoining lands as you don't want any unpleasant surprises down the road

-Any plans for the area, for example road widening schemes, published by the council or other statutory authorities

-Any compulsory purchase orders issued.

The zoning of adjoining land, plans for road widening or other developments like landfill dumps, will not show up in the title documents that your solicitor will receive, as he will only get title documents for the property you are purchasing.

Going out to a rural area and speaking to neighbours is also a good way to find out if any adverse developments are planned for the area.

If you are getting a site from a family member, this may not be necessary as you will almost certainly be very familiar with the area; otherwise, you need to carry out the enquiries and due diligence outlined above.

Chapter 4 Fees Involved in Buying Your Property

The fees which you will incur in buying or selling a property can really mount up and should not be overlooked or underestimated.

They can be broken down as follows:

-**Solicitor's professional fee**-this will vary from solicitor to solicitor, so shop around. The factors which will determine the legal fee include the value of the property, whether it is a land registry title or registry of deeds property, and some other issues.

In addition, your solicitor may charge you some miscellaneous charges in respect of postage, photocopying, faxes, etc., so check this when you are getting a quotation, and ensure that you are comparing like with like when getting quotations from different solicitors.

Some solicitors will waive these charges and allow for them in their professional fee.

When choosing a solicitor, don't overlook the personal relationship that can be extremely reassuring in a stressful time such as buying a property.

Being able to email or pick up the phone and speak directly with the solicitor handling your purchase will be a great comfort, even if it is only to see what is happening, ask a question, or seek some reassurance.

Having to get through secretaries and/or receptionists, who invariably act as "gate keepers", to speak to your solicitor will add to your stress if things are not going smoothly.

So, keep this in mind along with the fee and costs figure when making your mind up.

-Outlays Payable to Third Parties

There will also be outlays payable to 3rd parties.

This will include stamp duty to the Revenue Commissioners, land registry fees to the Property Registration Authority (PRA) for registration of ownership and to register the mortgage on your folio as a charge, commissioners' for oaths fees for swearing documents, and fees to law searchers who will carry out professional searches for closing against your folio, the vendors, and you to ensure that no judgments have been recently registered against you, the vendors, or the property.

The full range of Land registration fees can be accessed on the Property Registration Authority website.

However, the most common Land Registry fees are:

Application for registration of a transfer on sale where the value of the consideration is:

-not in excess of €50,000
    €400

-in excess of €50,000 and not in excess of €200,000
   €600

-in excess of €200,000 and not in excess of €400,000
   €700

-in excess of €400,000
   €800

Application for registration of a charge
   €175

Application for registration of a voluntary transfer
€130

Copy folio and map
   €40

So, if your house has a purchase price of €195,000, then your Land Registry fees will be €600 to register the transfer+€175 to register the mortgage/charge+€40 for a copy folio and map after the transfer has been completed.

You will also incur VAT on the solicitor's professional fee, and some of the miscellaneous charges.

The lender will also insist on a valuation being carried out on the property you propose to purchase, and will insist that you pay for this; in addition, you will have a fee for a surveyor/engineer/architect to carry out a structural survey and provide you with a report.

Both the fee for the valuation and structural survey will have to be paid by you.

Stamp Duty

Stamp duty is a tax on documents and most people's experience with stamp duty will be in relation to property purchase, which gives rise to the notion that stamp duty is applied to property.

But it is actually a tax on the instrument which witnesses the property transaction, and you will also see stamp duty applied to other instruments (legal documents) such as shares in companies.

Generally, stamp duty will be payable if the document/instrument is executed (signed) in Ireland, or if the transaction relates to property in the State.

You used to have 30 days within which to stamp your document/instrument with the Revenue Commissioners; this is now 44 days and your solicitor will do the stamping online with the new online stamping service provided by the Revenue Commissioners called eStamping.

The important thing from your perspective as a purchaser is to ensure to budget for your stamp duty, as you are the liable person for the stamp duty, and your solicitor will need the funds for stamp duty before the sale closes.

Residential Property

A much simplified stamp duty system was introduced in Ireland in 2010 with many of the previous exemptions and reliefs being abolished. However, there are reliefs still in existence including in relation to transfers between spouses, civil partners, and cohabitants.

Consanguinity relief for transfers or sites between certain related people has been slowly but surely removed by successive budgets, and is only available in certain limited circumstances.

So, check out your stamp duty liability before signing any contract or commencing to build on a site gifted to you as you do not want any unpleasant surprises.

The stamp duty rates in Ireland are as follows:

Residential Property

Up to €1,000,000-the rate is 1%

Excess over €1,000,000-the rate is 2%

TRANSFERS BETWEEN SPOUSES

Transfers between spouses are exempt from stamp duty.

For people buying their homes under local authority tenant purchase and similar schemes, a maximum amount of €100 is charged in stamp duty.

Chapter 5 The Physical Property, Getting a Structural Survey, and Planning issues

Ok, you have found the right house for you. And, yes, you are excited.

But you still need to keep your wits about you and there is no excuse for making this one stupid mistake when you are buying a property: failing to have a structural survey carried out.

This is one of the most important tasks for you to carry out.

And, when I say "structural survey" I mean a proper survey by an engineer or surveyor who has professional indemnity insurance. I do not mean a well-intentioned friend or relative who does a bit of building having a look and telling you, "Yes, it looks fine".

Because if your house subsequently discloses serious structural problems, you cannot sue your well-intentioned friend or relative.

And do not confuse a structural survey with the valuation report/survey which the lender will want carried out either. They are not the same thing, at all.

The reason for this is because of patent defects and latent defects and the fact that, legally, a purchaser is on constructive notice of any patent or latent defects of the property.

Patent defects are defects on title which are visible, or obvious from an inspection of the property eg a right of way.

Latent defects are defects which are not apparent from an inspection of the property, but which would become clear if enquiries and inspections were made which ought to have been made. This obligation would generally apply to your solicitor.

The statutory basis for this was the Conveyancing Act, 1882 which was repealed and the relevant section was re-enacted in the Land and Conveyancing Law Reform Act, 2009 which states:

"86.— (1) A purchaser is not affected prejudicially by notice of any fact, instrument, matter or thing unless—

(a) it is within the purchaser's own knowledge or would have come to the purchaser's knowledge if such inquiries and inspections had been made as ought reasonably to have been made by the purchaser, or

(b) in the same transaction with respect to which a question of notice to the purchaser arises, it has come to the knowledge of the purchaser's counsel, as such, or solicitor or other agent, as such, or would have come to the knowledge of the solicitor or other agent if such inquiries and inspections had been made as ought reasonably to have been made by the solicitor or agent."

So, to be protected as purchaser-and it is a well settled principle of law that a bona fide purchaser for value without notice acquires a good title to the property, unaffected by matters of which they had no notice, you and your solicitor must make reasonable "inquiries and inspections".

The Surveyor's Report

Your surveyor needs to do two things, at least:

1. Give a professional opinion on the structural integrity of the building, and flag up any issues which might occur later; this would include any signs of further investigation being required to establish that there is no pyrite in the building, for example, a close look at any cracks in the fabric of the property, signs of damp, etc;

2. Check that the property on the ground corresponds with the map of the property with the title deeds/on the Land Registry folio. In other words, that you are actually buying what you think you are buying.

It is also a good idea to ensure that your surveyor is going to check the Land Registry map versus the property as constructed on the ground. You may need to give him a copy of the folio map from the Land Registry folio, although he can also download this himself from the Property Registration Authority website (www.PRAI.ie), once he knows the folio number, which you can give him.

There is one further thing your surveyor should be able to do for you as part of his survey, and this generally applies to one off rural properties only.

Declaration of Identity

It may be necessary for him to provide a Declaration of Identity. This declaration is one which states that all of the necessary services-for example, septic tank and water well- for the property are located within the boundaries of the property.

You don't want to discover that your septic tank is located in a neighbouring field after you have moved in, or that the road leading up to your property is not a registered right of way over someone else's property.

Now, this will not be necessary if there is already a Declaration of Identity with the title documents. But there may not be, and your solicitor may request one from the Vendors of the property. The vendors may agree to provide this, by engaging their own surveyor to provide one.

Or they may say, 'no, that's a matter for you as purchaser'. If this is the case, and you are happy to have your own declaration drawn up, your surveyor is the ideal person to do this when he goes out to do his structural survey for you.

A surveyor's report will probably cost anything ranging from €200 up to €500 plus VAT.

It is money well spent, however, which can help you avoid a much more costly mistake which could come back to haunt you in later years eg a difficult boundary dispute with a neighbour, or the discovery that your septic tank is on someone else's property, or pyrite in the sub-floor of your house.

PYRITE

Pyrite in your property has the potential to break your heart and cause you catastrophic loss.

What is pyrite?

It is a common mineral that occurs in rocks. In particular circumstances, a chemical reaction, which creates expanding crystals within the material, can occur which causes the pyrite to swell causing the construction material in which the pyrite is present to expand, heave, crack and eventually crumble.

This problem occurs mostly in the floors of houses, causing huge problems for the property owner rendering the home virtually unsalable until the problem is resolved.

INDICATIONS OF PYRITE DAMAGE

Some tell tale signs include:

-Lifting of the floor slab resulting in cracking

-Cracking of floor finishes and tiles

-Doors catching on floors

-Horizontal cracking externally at damp proof course level

-Cracking on internal walls over doors

-Cracking of ground floor stud partitions and cracking of plasterboards.

Most, but by no means all, of the houses in Ireland where you will find problems with pyrite are located in North Leinster, and the Greater Dublin area including Meath, Offaly and Kildare. The reason for this is the use of stone from quarries in this area which contain framboidal pyrite.

IS 398, published by the NSAI in 2013, aims to set new standards in relation to pyrite by providing protocols for testing and categorization, and setting out a methodology for remediation works.

IS 398 provides for 3 certificates in relation to the presence or absence of pyrite in the underfloor hardcore of a house:

1. Green means it is pyrite free

2. Amber means the hardcore is susceptible to limited or significant expansion and monitoring of the damage is required

3. Red means you have a pyrite problem and the stone infill in the floor of the house will have to be removed and replaced. This involves the removal of the floor slab, insulation and damp proof membrane. The replacement stone and remedial works should also be certified in accordance with IS 398.

Buying Your New Home

As indicated previously, and I make no apology for labouring the point because it is crucial, when buying a house you should make sure to have a structural survey carried out first.

Then, your engineer should be able to advise you whether further investigation is necessary to be sure about the position in relation to pyrite, and that it is not present in your house.

You may have to insist that you are provided by the vendor with a report from an accredited laboratory confirming that the property is pyrite free before proceeding with your purchase, especially if the house is in one of the areas where pyrite is a problem.

This testing will involve the taking of core samples from the floor of the house, and a delay of about 3 or 4 weeks as much of the testing is carried out in laboratories in the UK. But it is strongly advisable if your engineer tells you that further investigation is necessary.

If in any doubt, discuss this with both your engineer and solicitor because the consequences of buying a property with a pyrite problem are very serious, and it will be difficult to sell without expensive and disturbing remedial work being carried out by you.

Let me tell you a little cautionary tale: in 2014, a client of mine had gone sale agreed to purchase a repossessed property. I strongly advised her, as I do everybody, to have a structural survey carried out.

She agreed and the surveyor soon produced his report, Now, because the property was repossessed, the property was sadly lacking some care and attention, but that was to be expected and the price was right.

However, the report also raised some questions about the particular type of cracking evident in the property and raised the question of pyrite. So, I told the vendor bank's solicitor that we would need to see a report from an independent laboratory confirming that the house was pyrite free.

Initially, the bank refused. But we dug our heels in and insisted on it. The bank then arranged the pyrite test to be carried out, and when the results came back from the UK some 6 weeks later, the report confirmed that there was-surprise, surprise-pyrite in the house.

This led to another bout of negotiations about price with the price of remedial works-€20,000-€40,000-being knocked off the price. As it turned out, agreement could not be reached on how much would be allowed for this remedial work and the purchase did not go ahead.

CONCLUSION RE YOUR SURVEY

Don't be afraid to ask your surveyor plenty of questions, especially if there is anything in the report which may cause you concern, or which you do not understand.

Quite frankly, you should try to get his replies in writing, for example by email.

The first thing you will see in most surveyor's report will be a heavy disclaimer.

Nevertheless, he should have professional indemnity insurance and be a be member of one of the professional bodies, so he cannot step aside from his professional obligation to you, and his duty of care, with a strong disclaimer.

PLANNING

Planning is another significant area which must be checked carefully when buying a property. Your solicitor will do this for you, but you can make your own enquiries too.

Both you and your surveyor should be on the lookout for any work which has been carried out recently, and which might require planning permission.

Remember: your solicitor will not be visiting the property; he only deals with the legal documents of title, planning documents, and other documents. You and the surveyor will visit the house, at least once so you may spot a fresh extension or conversion job which may or may not require planning, but almost certainly requires further enquiry. So, let your solicitor know.

The old truism in relation to property is: "the day you buy is the day you sell".

If you buy a property with a serious problem to do with planning, and you are unable to resolve it, you will have a serious difficulty selling your property.

BACKGROUND TO PLANNING IN IRELAND

The first significant planning law in Ireland was the Local Government (Planning and Development) Act, 1963.

The next major piece of legislation dealing with development and planning was the Local Government (Planning and Development) Act, 2000 which consolidated Irish planning law by incorporating 9 planning and development acts passed since 1963.

The Local Government (Planning and Development) Act, 2000 was itself amended by the Planning and Development (Amendment) Act 2002 and the Planning and Development (Strategic Infrastructure) Act, 2003.

The Act at section 4(2) (a) provided for planning regulations, the main one now in force being the Planning and Development Regulations 2001.

Planning Register

Section 7 of the Local Government (Planning and Development) Act, 2000 provides for a planning register to be kept by a planning authority (section 2(1)). However there is no guarantee that the planning register is kept up to date by the authority as they may do so "as soon as may be".

When your solicitor is acting for you in the purchase of a property, he should have a planning register search carried out before allowing you sign the contract for sale.

Development

Development is defined in section 3(1) of the 2000 Act as:

"3.—(1) In this Act, "development" means, except where the context otherwise requires, the carrying out of any works on, in, over or under land or the making of any material change in the use of any structures or other land."

So there are 2 separate parts to "development" as defined:

1. Carrying out of works and

2. Material change of use.

However, unauthorised developments can only have taken place after 1st October 1964.

Exempted Development

Exempted development is development where an applicant is exempt from the obligation to obtain planning permission which occurs in 3 circumstances:

1. Where the development took place before 1st of October, 1964;

2. Where section 4 of Local Government (Planning and Development) Act, 2000 provides that certain types of development are exempt;

3. Where the Minister made regulations providing classes of development to be exempt, which he did under the Local Government (Planning and Development) Act, 2000 and the Local Government (Planning and Development) Act, 1963.

One of the most important categories of exemption is contained in the 2000 Act and includes:

1. a) where development consists of carrying out works which affect only the interior of the structure and

2. b) works which does not materially affect the external appearance of the structure.

From a solicitor's perspective, he will need to get an architect to furnish a Certificate or Declaration confirming that particular work is exempt, if that is claimed, and the grounds which bring the development under an exempt category.

Planning Permission

Planning permission is required for all development of land carried out since 1st October 1964 and which is not exempted development or for the retention of unauthorised structures.

Part III of the Local Government (Planning and Development) Act, 2000 deals with planning permission, and sets out the procedure for applying for permission, time periods, notices, and gives the planning authority the power to impose conditions when granting permission.

Your solicitor needs to read all conditions imposed in any planning permission and must ensure that any financial condition imposed in relation to the development has been complied with.

ENFORCEMENT

Part VIII of the Act provides for enforcement mechanisms including

1. Criminal prosecution

2. An enforcement notice under section 154/5 of the Act

3. A planning injunction under section 160 of the Local Government (Planning and Development) Act, 1963.

3 VITAL QUESTIONS FOR YOU AND YOUR SOLICITOR

Critical questions to be answered in relation to the property are

1. Has there been, in relation to the property, any development (including change of use or exempted development) within the meaning of the Planning Acts on or after the 1st October 1964.

2. Is there evidence of compliance with the financial conditions by way of letter/receipt from the Local Authority.

3. Is there a Certificate/Opinion from an Architect/Engineer that the Permission/Approval relates to the property and that the development has been carried out in conformity with the Permission/Approval and with the Building Bye-Law Approval (if applicable) and that all conditions other than financial conditions have been complied with.

If there is formal confirmation from the local authority that the roads and services have been taken in charge, this is acceptable that the financial contributions and/or lodgement of bonds with the council have been complied with.

BUILDING CONTROL REGULATIONS

The Building Control Act, 1990 is the important Act here, and provided for building regulations to be drawn up to ensure buildings were built in accordance with the best Code of Practice. The main provisions of this act came into force on 1stJune, 1992.

A Certificate/Opinion of Compliance with building regulations from an architect/engineer is essential when you are buying a property. There should be no reservations or exceptions in it.

THE BUILDING REGULATIONS

The Building Control Act, 1990, and the Regulations made under it, are "the Building Regulations". Prior to the Building Regulations some, but not all, parts of the country had building bye-laws.

The Building Control Act, 1990 did away with the need to obtain bye-law approval from 1st June, 1992. If no notice was served before 1st December 1992 in respect of works carried out prior to 13th December 1989 the works are deemed to have been carried out in accordance with the bye-law.

From 1st June, 1992 the Building Regulations apply in relation to works carried out, and this includes alterations or extensions of existing buildings.

The Building Regulations set out a new system to regulate building practice in Ireland and to improve building standards.

In a similar way to the Planning Acts, the Building Control Act, 1990, provided that certain classes of development are exempt.

For all works and uses to which the Building Regulations apply a commencement notice must be submitted to the building control authority.

The Building Control Regulations 1997 provide for the need for a fire safety certificate to be obtained before work commences on a development. Domestic dwellings are exempt and there is a list of other exemptions also.

There is a limit of 5 years from completion of the works or change of use after which no enforcement notice may be served by the local planning authority.

Architect's Certificates of Compliance

It is essential that your property has a certificate of compliance with planning permission and building regulations from an architect/engineer.

Your solicitor will ensure this and the certificate of compliance should

1. Contain the qualifications of the person giving the certificate

2. Confirm the means of knowledge

3. Confirm that the planning permission relates to the development in sale

4. Confirm that the design conforms with the Building Regulations

5. Confirm that the development complies with the planning permission

6. Not contain any qualifications or exceptions which are not generally acceptable

7. Be dated and signed.

Certifiers may also be asked for a copy of their professional indemnity insurance to confirm the adequacy of same.

Your solicitor will also need to be careful about the difference between a Notification of a Decision to Grant Permission/Approval, and the actual planning permission which is the Notification of Grant of Permission/Approval.

Checklist for Planning Documentation

Here are 5 things that your solicitor will need to check in relation to planning documentation:

1. Is it a final grant and not just a notification of a decision to grant?

2. Does it relate to the property you are buying?

3. What is the expiry date of the permission? (A planning permission generally lasts for 5 years).

4. Was the development carried out within the lifespan of the permission?

5. Take a close look at the conditions of the permission, especially the financial conditions (if any).

The key questions he needs to ask when acting for you as buyer are:

1. Is there planning permission?

2. Were building regulations or building bye-laws complied with?

3. Is there an architect's certificate confirming compliance with planning permission and building regulations/building bye-laws?

You as purchaser have enough to be worrying about without worrying about planning issues. And you can rely on your solicitor to do that work on your behalf.

But do remember that you may be able to provide him with some assistance because your solicitor will never see the property, and you will, probably many times. So, if there is a new extension or an unusual arrangement for the disposal of sewerage for example, it would be prudent to mention it to your solicitor.

More often than not, this will not be necessary.

But it will be your house after all and probably the biggest financial investment you will make in your life.

BER Certs and Reports

A Building Energy Rating (BER) Certificate is an indication of the energy performance of a home. A BER certificate is accompanied by an Advisory Report which identifies how you might improve the energy performance of your home. It's similar to the energy label for a household electrical appliance like your fridge. The label has a scale of A-G. A-rated homes are the most energy efficient and will tend to have the lowest energy bills.

A BER is compulsory for all homes offered for sale or rent. A BER is also required before a new home is occupied for the first time. Advertisements must include BER details when a home is offered for sale or rent.

BER assessments are completed by registered BER Assessors who have been trained under the National Framework of Qualifications, passed the SEAI BER Assessor exam and have registered with SEAI.

A BER is required under the following circumstances:

-The home owner must obtain a BER before a new home is occupied for the first time regardless of whether it is offered for sale or rent.

-When a new or existing home is offered for sale or rent the seller / renter must provide a BER to prospective buyers or tenants. BER details must be included in advertisements when a home is offered for sale or rent.

BER assessments performed on new homes also help determine compliance to Part L of the Building Regulations.

Chapter 6   Conveyancing-The Legal Stuff

What is conveyancing?

"Conveyancing" is the legal term for the transfer of legal title to "real property" (real estate) from one party to another.

GOOD MARKETABLE TITLE

One thing your solicitor will need to ensure is that you get "good marketable title" to the property. As the old saying goes in relation to property: "the day you buy is the day you sell".

Many lending institutions will not advance monies where the title being offered as security is not going to be good marketable title and where the solicitor is going to have to "qualify title".

"Title" when speaking about property is evidence of ownership of a particular person of an interest or estate in property.

"Good title" is where a vendor of property can prove that they are the legal owner of a certain estate or interest in a property. Note that 2 or more people could have an estate/interest in a property, for example, a freehold owner and a leasehold owner in respect of the same property.

"Good marketable title" is not statutorily defined. However it means the standard of title which is given and accepted by conveyancing solicitors following good conveyancing practice and rules set out by the Law Society of Ireland.

A "certificate of title" is an approved (by the Law Society of Ireland) form of certificate of title which is accepted by lending institutions arising from prudent standards of conveyancing in Ireland.

This would include, amongst other things,

-The use of the standard Law Society of Ireland contract for sale (2009 edition is the current one)

-Investigation of title is carried out using the Law Society approved Objections and Requisitions at a minimum

-A freehold title or

-Leasehold title with at least 70 years unexpired or

-If a Land Registry leasehold title, it must be either "absolute" or "good" leasehold.

This "certificate of title" system only applies to residential property conveyancing.

It allows the lender to permit the solicitor for the purchaser to investigate title and also gives responsibility to the solicitor for having the mortgage registered in the bank's favour and secured on the property.

CERTIFICATE OF TITLE SYSTEM

The Certificate of Title System obliges the purchaser's solicitor to give an undertaking and a certificate to the lender in a format agreed between the Law Society and the lenders. The undertaking and certificate of title are provided by the solicitor in his capacity as the borrower's solicitor; he does not act for the lender.

In practice, once the loan is approved for the purchaser, the documentation containing the blank solicitor's undertaking form and certificate of title form, together with the loan offer and mortgage deed are sent to the purchaser's solicitor.

The lender will only release the loan cheque when it has received the solicitor's undertaking. This undertaking obliges the solicitor acting for the purchaser to ensure that

1. The purchaser is acquiring good marketable title to the property

2. The mortgage documentation is completed properly and signed by the borrower

3. The mortgage ranks as a first legal charge on the property

4. All necessary documentation is properly stamped and registered in the Registry of Deeds or Land Registry

5. All documentation including certificate of title is furnished to the lender once the change of ownership has been registered.

Qualifying the Solicitor's Undertaking

In some circumstances, for example where the solicitor is not able to obtain "good marketable title" perhaps due to a planning difficulty with the property, the solicitor will have to qualify his/her undertaking.

If this is necessary, it will have to be cleared in advance with the lender as the bank may not agree to it and may withdraw the loan offer.

This could also arise in an estate where the estate has not yet been taken in charge by the local authority and the indemnity from the original builder is of no value as he has been dissolved.

THE FAMILY HOME

One of the things that your solicitor will be concerned about, and needs to make enquiries about, is whether the property is a family home.

To do this, your solicitor will obtain a statutory declaration from the vendors setting out the status of the property vis a vis family law legislation in Ireland.

The Family Home Protection Act, 1976 prevents one spouse, in whose sole name the family home was vested, from dealing with the property without the knowledge and/or consent of the non-owning spouse.

There is no differentiation between husband or wife, when it comes to protecting the non owning spouse.

So, the prior written consent of any non-owning spouse must be obtained prior to any conveyance of the family home since 1976.

However, section 54 of the Family Law Act, 1995 imposes a six year time limit within which proceedings must be taken by the non-owning spouse to have a conveyance declared void:

Proceedings shall not be instituted to have a conveyance declared void by reason only of subsection (1) after the expiration of 6 years from the date of the conveyance.

EXCEPTIONS

There are four exceptions provided for in section 3(1) above:

1. Agreements made in contemplation of marriage

2. Conveyance to a bona fide purchaser for full value (the purchaser must act in good faith-this means that the purchaser must make proper and reasonable enquiries and inspections to ascertain the position. This means that a solicitor acting for a purchaser must carry out all necessary investigations to clarify the position concerning the family home. Failure to do so will leave his client open to a challenge from the non-owning spouse)

3. Conveyance of an interest by a person/body other than a spouse (e.g. mortgagee bank/lender)

4. Where a Court orders the sale of the home in a judicial separation.

You will note from the exceptions above that you, as purchaser, will be protected once you are a bona fide purchaser for full value, and your solicitor carries out the necessary investigations.

WHAT IS A FAMILY HOME?

A family home is defined in the Family Home Protection Act, 1976 is a dwelling in which a married couple ordinarily resides. However, a family home also includes the former residence of a couple who are separated as well as the current home of a married couple.

It also includes a dwelling in which a spouse is residing having been forced to leave the family home by the other spouse.

Prior Written Consent

Where the property being sold is jointly owned by a married couple, no spousal consent is required to a conveyance.

The spousal consent must be prior to the purported conveyance and must be in writing.

It is also important that the consent is informed-the spouse must know what he/she is consenting to.

The need for spousal consent can be dispensed with by a Court in certain circumstances (section 4(1), Family Home Protection Act, 1976).

Generally, this occurs where a spouse is unreasonably withholding consent.

The Family Home Protection Act, 1976, the Judicial Separation and Family Law Reform Act, 1989 and the Family Law (Divorce) Act, 1996 grant powers to Court to deal with the family home which it does by way of property adjustment orders and/or orders for the sale of the family home.

Systems of Registration of Ownership of Property

Once you have bought the property your ownership will be registered in the appropriate register by your solicitor.

There are 2 systems of registration of property in Ireland:

-the Registry of Deeds and

-the Land Registry.

They both fall under the umbrella of the Property Registration Authority.

Registries of Deeds properties tend to be in urban areas, for example Dublin, and the important thing to understand about these properties is that it deals with registration of documents, not registration of title.

The Land Registry, on the other hand, deals with registration of title, not just documents, and the State then guarantees the title to these properties.

Land Registry Documents

Land registry documents comprise a folio of a property which is in 3 parts:

1. part 1 gives details of the property and a map reference

2. part 2 gives the registered owner and class of title

3. part 3 lists the burdens on the title eg mortgages/charges, rights of way, right to reside, etc.

Ownership of land registry property is transferred by a deed of transfer, but title only passes when the transfer has been registered in Land Registry.

TYPES OF OWNERSHIP

One thing you need to be crystal clear about, if you are buying with another person, is whether you will buy as joint tenants or tenants in common.

Spouses will buy as joint tenants, and the default position at Land Registry is for joint ownership to be held as a joint tenancy, but if you are buying with a friend or partner, you will want to think about this and discuss with your friend/partner how you are to hold the property.

The difference is as follows: a joint tenancy means that if Mick and Susan purchase a property together, and share ownership as joint tenants, then if either one of them dies, the property passes as a matter of law by survivorship to the other party.

However, if Mick and Susan bought as tenants in common, then if either one dies his/her share will go to whoever he/she chooses, eg a family member.

Bear in mind that even though these terms-tenants in common/joint tenants-use words that are understood by virtually everyone who understands English, they have a slightly different meaning when used as legal terms and in the context of property ownership.

A joint tenancy means that each owner has an equal undivided share which passes automatically on the death of the joint tenant to the remaining joint tenant(s). A joint tenancy cannot be passed under a will, as if falls outside the will.

A tenancy in common can pass under a will or in an intestacy situation and the shares in a tenancy in common do not have to be equal.

STAGES IN A CONVEYANCE

For many purchasers, one of the most stressful things is the apparent slowness of the process. Frustration and stress is, therefore, perfectly understandable.

If you have ever bought or sold property in Ireland-be it commercial or residential-it will have seemed to be a very slow process.

And it can seem like it goes on forever.

A smooth, fast conveyance can be completed in about 5 weeks, start to finish. However, it is typically a bit longer-realistically you would want to allow 8 weeks- and in some unfortunate situations, it can take longer again.

But there are some very good reasons for an apparent 'slowness' in the completion of the transaction. (Quite frankly, on some occasions there are no excuses whatsoever!)

Ending up with a poor title to your property or a title that will be unacceptable to your lender will lead to significant and serious problems.

This is the prime reason for the apparent slowness of the process, and your solicitor will need to be extremely careful to obtain all the necessary documents of title, planning documents, receipts for payment of local property tax, household charge, NPPR (non principal private residence) tax (where appropriate), and so on.

The most important factors to be considered, and tasks to be carried out, by your legal advisors include those relating to

-Planning

-Financing

-Family home legislation

-Acceptable title (good marketable title)

-Searches for judgments etc.

-Registration with Land Registry or Registry of Deeds

-Stamp duty and capital gains tax

-Contract for sale special conditions

-Completion of sale and any problems arising at closing or post completion.

These are the most important factors to be taken care of by your solicitor, depending on whether you are buying or selling.

It never ceases to amaze me how many people seek to cut corners when it comes to legal fees in their property purchase/sale.

So, what's involved in a conveyance?

There are five stages in a conveyance:

1. Pre contract

2. Contract

3. Post contract/pre closing

4. Closing

5. Post completion.

VENDOR'S SOLICITOR

The vendor's solicitor will need to take the following steps:

-Check the seller's title to the property. This will involve taking up the title deeds, either from a lending institution or the vendor.

-Check what sort of property is being sold eg residential home, commercial premises, licensed premises, etc.

-Check that planning is in order for the property

-Check the Family Home status of the property (if appropriate), and if it is held in sole ownership, to obtain the prior written consent of the spouse, if there is one

-Ascertain whether the seller has received any notices which affect the property (eg from a local authority re compulsory purchase)

-Check outgoings eg rates, local authority charges, local property tax, management company fees, and so on

-Decide whether a capital gains tax certificate is necessary (where the price is in excess of €500,000)

-Check whether there are any flaws in the title to the property

-Give the vendor a 'section 68' letter setting out costs and outlay which will arise

-Prepare the contract for sale

-Reply to requisitions on title (see below)

-Draft the Family Law declaration setting out the position re the Family Home Protection Act, 1976

-Check the position re outgoings for the property and see that they will be discharged prior to closing

-Arrange for closing of the sale

-Find out what mortgage is outstanding on the property to ensure discharge of same once funds are received from the purchaser's solicitor

-Discharge any undertakings given on closing

PURCHASER'S SOLICITOR

The purchaser's solicitor will need to:

-Read the contract and related documentation, particularly planning documents, check the title, and any special conditions in the contract

-Advise the purchaser to have a full structural survey on the property carried out because when buying a second hand property the principle of "caveat emptor" (buyer beware) applies

-Advise on tax such as stamp duty which will be payable and ascertain whether there are any tax reliefs available

-Advise the purchaser to take out insurance as the property may be underinsured or not at all and if the purchaser is taking out a mortgage the lender will want evidence that insurance is in place prior to releasing the loan cheque

-Make pre contract enquiries including planning

-If the contract is to be made subject to loan approval, check the relevant clause in the contract providing for this

-If the contract is to be made subject to a satisfactory structural survey, draft the required clause for inclusion in contract

-Give the purchaser a section 68 letter setting out his fees, outlays, and costs which will be incurred

-Ensure purchaser has loan approval

-Get the purchaser to sign the contract, assuming everything above is in order

-Raise requisitions and objections (if any) on title

-Setting out the closing documentation required and furnishing same to the vendor's solicitor

-Check the lending institutions requirements and complete and furnish the required documentation

-Draft the deed of transfer to transfer the interest in the property to the purchaser

-Decide on and requisition all searches to be carried out

-Ensure finance will be in place to close the sale

-Ensure stamp duty is paid and have the transfer registered either in Land Registry or Registry of Deeds.

Caveat Emptor

The doctrine of "caveat emptor" ("buyer beware") is an important one to understand when you are buying a property. It refers to the physical description of the property and the fact that, as you are buying a second hand property and have every opportunity to inspect the property fully, you must carry out prudent enquiries to ensure you know what your are getting.

You must satisfy yourself as to the boundaries and condition of the property. This is why you should have a full structural survey carried out prior to signing the contract, and why I keep repeating this advice ad nauseam.

Bear in mind that the vendor is not under a duty to disclose any physical defects in the property. Certainly, he cannot mislead or lie to you. But he can stay quiet and say nothing.

The purchaser's solicitor needs to

-check that he/she can acquire good marketable title on behalf of the purchaser

-check that the title being provided is contracted for in the contract for sale

-check the property in the contract is properly and adequately identified in the title documents.

These steps in the conveyancing process in Ireland are designed to ensure that a purchaser is not obliged to go to the cost of carrying out a full investigation of the title being offered before the vendor is legally obliged to sell.

1. PRE CONTRACT ENQUIRIES

Prior to contracts becoming binding the purchasers' solicitor will raise "pre contract enquiries".

These pre contract enquiries are vitally important to ensure that you are not bound to a contract which you will later regret.

Pre-contract enquiries should deal also with the physical location and condition of the property, including access to the property, planning, water supply, and other services.

Other matters raised will include roads, footpath water, sewerage, gas, electricity, refuse charges/bin charges- to the property, local property tax or other charges affecting the property, what contents are included, the BER certificate and report to see what energy rating the property has, whether any work has been carried out which will require planning, etc.

It is only when contracts are exchanged and binding on both parties-that is, signed by both parties- that full examination of the title is carried out by the purchaser's solicitor. This helps reduce legal costs for you as purchaser, and saves time expended by the purchaser's solicitor.

Full examination of the legal title to the property is carried out by your solicitor raising standard "Objections and Requisitions on Title". These are standard queries and requests raised in respect of the vendor's title, and other matters relevant to the property being sold.

The standard documentation used in a conveyancing transaction in Ireland are

> -the Law Society Contract for Sale (current version is 2009 one) and
> -Objections and Requisitions on Title.

2. BOOKING DEPOSIT AND CONTRACT DEPOSIT

I've mentioned already, in dealing with the auctioneer, the paying over of a booking deposit. This, as you know, is refundable if the sale does not go ahead.

However, a contract deposit is not, and once you have paid it over, it is not refundable unless the vendor does not sign the contract in which case there is no binding contract. Let me explain.

The vendor's solicitor will issue a contract of sale at the outset together with supporting title documentation. Your solicitor will raise pre contract enquiries-that is, before you sign the contract. Once he is satisfied with the replies and with the special conditions in the contract, and knows you have finance arranged, he will invite you in to his office to sign the contract.

At this stage you also have to pay the contract deposit. So, let's say the price of the house is €195,000. The contract deposit will be 10% which is €19,500. You will already have paid a booking deposit to the auctioneer-say €5,000. Then the balance payable on signing the contract is €14,500.

This is the balance of the contract deposit and is sent back with the contract in duplicate to the vendor's solicitor. From a legal perspective, this is only an offer to buy on your behalf.

3. CONTRACT

It is only when the vendor signs the contracts and sends one copy back to your solicitor that there is a binding contract in place and both solicitors then work towards closing the sale.

But once there is a binding contract in place, you are committed to completing and your contract deposit is not refundable. As there is a binding contract in place, you could also be sued to complete the sale.

4. CLOSING/COMPLETION

Your solicitor will pay over the balance of the purchase money on closing provided he receives all the closing documentation he has requested, and provided the legal searches are clear-that is, that there are no judgments or orders affecting the property or the vendors. (If you are borrowing, you will also be searched against too by the legal searchers).

Once the closing bank draft is handed over in exchange for the closing documents and explained, "clear" searches, the keys to the property will be handed over to your solicitor, or the auctioneer will be instructed to release the keys to you.

Conflicts of Interest-Acting for Both Parties in a Conveyance

It used to be the case that a solicitor in a small number of circumstances could act for both parties to a conveyance. However new regulations contained in a 2012 Statutory Instrument, S.I. No. 375/2012 – Solicitors (Professional Practice, Conduct and Discipline – Conveyancing Conflict of Interest) Regulation 2012, has restricted this even more and it is now possible in only very limited circumstances.

This situation occurs frequently when someone is being given a site by a family member to allow the construction of a house. In this situation, both you as recipient and the donor will need your own solicitor.

If you are in this fortunate situation, being the recipient of a gift of a site, you might want to consider discharging all costs of the transaction.

Checklist for Purchaser of Residential Property

The checklist below is a useful one for your solicitor to use when acting for you as purchaser.

It will also give you a useful check list of many of the questions your solicitor will be asking you, and some of the other details you will need to take care of, so that they do not come as a surprise to you.

1. Details of the Vendor

Name

Address

Price

Deposit

Loan

Solicitor for vendor

2. Finance

Deposit/equity from sale of property

Loan

Amount

Name of lending institution

Branch/address

Loan application status

Structural survey/fire cover/life cover

Bridging?

Loan pack from bank?

3. Items included in Sale

Inventory

Value

4. Purchase of Part of Folio?

Map

Easements including rights of way/right to light/services/maintenance

5. Structural Survey

Inspection by expert independent of lending institution

Valuer's report for lending institution

6. Planning

Planning search before signing contract-check local planning office

Change in planning?

Change of use/intensification of use?

Fire certificate/building regulations?

7. Insurance

Cover from date of signing contract

Life cover?

Mortgage protection?

Closing day-what happens on closing day?

A question I am regularly asked by my property clients is "what happens on closing day?"

Closing day, or completion day, is the day that the property is finally handed over from vendor to purchaser. The vendor must hand over the keys of the house and vacant possession.

Prior to this the vendors' solicitor will almost certainly have sent, by registered post or DX, all documents of title to the purchasers' solicitor for completion. These documents are sent on the basis that they will be held strictly in trust and to the order of the vendors' solicitor. This means nothing can be done with them until the vendors' solicitor gives approval.

The purchasers' solicitor must ensure that all the closing funds are transferred by electronic funds transfer to the client bank account of the vendors' solicitor.

Legal Searches

The purchasers' solicitor will also order legal searches for closing day, and will check them once they are received and send them on to the vendors' solicitor to be certified and/or explained.

The purpose of these legal searches is to ensure that no judgments or judgment mortgages, or other burdens, have been registered against the vendors or the property between the date of signing the contract and completion day.

Once the purchasers' solicitor has received all closing documents of title and satisfactory explanations, if necessary, for the searches he will authorise the vendors' solicitor to release the purchase funds.

At the same time the vendors' solicitor will authorise the release of the title documents and let the auctioneer know that he can release the keys.

Closing Day Inspection

Before the above sequence of events happens, however, you would be well advised to carry out a final inspection of the property, just before your funds are released.

Occasionally, I have seen problems on closing day such as a lot of rubbish left by the buyers when they have finished emptying out their house, or even the removal of some contents that the purchasers thought were part of the deal.

It is easy to assume that certain things which are built in or stuck to the ground are included in the sale, but it is always better to check the contents listing carefully in the contract when you are signing it, and to check the condition of the house just before you get the keys and your solicitor releases the money to the other solicitor.

It is much easier to resolve problems when the money has not been handed over, rather than after.

Hopefully, you now have a clearer idea of what to expect on closing day, regardless of whether you are a buyer or seller.

Chapter 7 Booking deposits and contract deposits

When purchasing property in Ireland you need to understand that you will pay two deposits:

1. A booking deposit to the auctioneer

2. The contract deposit

The Booking Deposit

The booking deposit you pay to an auctioneer is fully refundable. You can change your mind about buying the house for good, bad, or no reason and you are entitled to get your booking deposit back.

Just make sure the booking deposit is paid to the auctioneer, not the vendor, and get a receipt confirming it is a booking deposit. You can also, if you feel it necessary, visit the website of the Property Services Regulatory Authority and check the auctioneer is on the public register.

The Contract Deposit

The contract deposit is payable when you sign and return the contracts to the vendor's solicitor.

Let's assume you are buying a property for €200,000. The contract deposit will be 10% of the purchase price-that is, €20,000.

So, when you sign the contracts you will have to pay €20,000 less whatever booking deposit you have paid to the auctioneer.

Let's assume you have paid €5,000 booking deposit to the auctioneer; then you will have to pay €15,000 when you are signing and returning the contracts.

Once the vendor has signed the contracts and returns one part to your solicitor there is a binding contract in place. At this point you will not get your deposit back if you change your mind.

However, there is an exception to this: if your solicitor had inserted a "subject to finance" clause in the contract and the finance does not, for whatever reason, come through then you may be entitled to the deposit back on the basis that there is no binding contract in place as the contract was "subject to finance".

Be very careful, though: failure to complete a sale can lead to the forfeiting of your deposit.

Also, the vendor can actually sue you for the balance of the purchase price and to compel you to complete the sale-a remedy of specific performance. This will not be of much use, however, if you are simply unable to complete.

But damages will be payable if the vendor rescinds the contract by serving a Completion Notice and you are unable to complete (see below).

In addition, the vendor can sell the property to someone else and if they get a lower price he can sue you for the difference-that is, the drop in value or sales price. First, he needs to serve a Completion Notice on you.

Stakeholder

The vendor's solicitor holds the contract deposit as 'stakeholder'. This means he/she is personally responsible to both purchaser and vendor for its safe-keeping. The stakeholder cannot hand over the deposit to the vendor until the vendor is entitled to it.

Completion Notice

Once the closing date has passed and you have been unable to complete the purchase the vendor can serve a Completion Notice on you. This makes time of the essence in relation to completing the sale.

When the time in the Completion Notice has passed the vendor can rescind (bring to an end) the contract and pursue you for damages and loss arising from your failure to complete the transaction.

Buying at Auction

When you buy at auction the procedure is slightly different. When the hammer falls and you are the highest bidder you will not be paying a booking deposit, but will have to sign the contract and pay the contract deposit.

If you are unable to complete, therefore, you will lose your deposit.

So, you need to carry out all your research about the property you have your eye on before you go to the auction; doing so later on is too late and is a stupid, avoidable mistake. (Learn more about buying property at auction here).

Conclusion

Booking deposits are refundable; contract deposits are not so get professional advice and carry out your due diligence before signing the contract and paying the contract deposit, not after.

Chapter 8 Buying an Apartment

Buying an apartment, or a townhouse which is part of a mixed residential/commercial development, which involves a management company looking after common areas of an estate, is different from buying a house.

When you buy a house, you will have your own front door, perhaps a garden (front and/or back), and there will be a road and footpaths servicing your house. You are responsible for your own property, your gardens, the roof of your house, and so on.

But if you live in an apartment block there will only be one roof and you will probably have a large number of apartments in the same building.

So, a management company will be appointed to look after the apartment block and the other common areas-for example stairs, lifts, halls, landings etc.-and each apartment owner will be a member of the management company and pay annual management fees. The management company will also take out a block insurance policy on the block and ensure that the interest of each apartment owner, and their lender if there is one, is noted on the block policy.

So, there are 3 main differences between buying a house and buying an apartment in Ireland:

1. the title to an apartment is always leasehold, unlike the freehold title of a house,

2. an apartment will involve common areas as it will be part of a building scheme

3. an apartment will involve a management company to manage the common areas eg stairs, entrance, lift, security, etc.

A lease is always required for an apartment because it allows the entering into mutual covenants by the apartment owners and the management company for the benefit of all apartment owners.

For example, the apartment owners will covenant to pay the management company fee and agree to restrictions for harmonious communal living with their neighbours, and the management company will covenant to maintain the common areas.

These covenants and conditions can be enforced on later owners of the apartments.

Prior to the enactment of the Land and Conveyancing Law Reform Act, 2009 there was a difficulty in enforcing covenants against later purchasers of freehold land.

This is no longer the case with the passing of the Land and Conveyancing Law Reform Act, 2009.

PARTIES TO THE LEASE

There are generally 3 parties to the lease:

-the lessor (developer/builder)

-the lessee (apartment owner)

-the management company.

A fourth party could be a lender who has a charge over the land.

THE APARTMENT PROPERTY

The lease of an apartment will transfer a cube of space including the surfaces of floors, ceilings and walls but excluding all structural parts. It may also include a balcony, patio or car parking space but these are more commonly excluded with an exclusive licence granted to the apartment purchaser.

This allows the Management Company and lessor to retain control of these areas and the management company is responsible for maintenance and repairs of the block, and will need to set up a sinking fund to provide for the maintenance of the building.

The lease for the apartment will contain a provision for a nominal rent with a provision for a rent review. This prevents the apartment owner from buying out the ground rent which would end the lease and break up the relationship between lessor and lessee.

THE LEASE COVENANTS

There are 3 main covenants in an apartment lease:

1. a covenant by the lessee to perform certain obligations, the most important of which are to pay the service charge and

comply with the rules and regulations of the management company;

2. a covenant by the lessor to provide certain services, the most important of which is to maintain the apartment building and the common areas which includes insuring the building against the usual risks and public liability insurance in respect of the common areas, maintain proper books of account, and take steps to enforce performance of the lessees' obligations under the leases;

3. a covenant by the management company to provide the same services once the management company agreement has been completed and the common areas transferred over to it.

THE MANAGEMENT SCHEME AND MANAGEMENT COMPANY

A scheme for the management of the common areas will be put in place which will be implemented by a management company specifically set up for this purpose.

What typically happens is the developer sets up the management company and signs a contract with the management company for the transfer of the common areas to the company. Each apartment owner then becomes a member of the management company as he/she purchases an apartment.

Once all the apartments have been sold the developer transfers the common areas to the management company, which is ultimately controlled by the apartment owners.

PURCHASING A SECOND HAND APARTMENT

As an apartment purchaser is only purchasing a "cube of space" she needs to be certain that she has access to the apartment and other appropriate "easements" from the lessor or management company.

A surveyor carrying out a survey for the purchase of an apartment should also check out the entire building because the new apartment owner will be contributing with her service charge to a fund for the repair and maintenance of the common areas.

The management company will generally appoint a managing agent whose job it is to put in place a block insurance policy to insure the whole block, and manage the estate including common areas, lifts, stairs, possibly green areas, any play area, car parking, etc.

The managing agent's job is to ensure, on behalf of the management company, that the estate is well maintained and managed for the benefit of all apartment owners. This ensures harmonious living and a sound investment which is much more likely to appreciate in value.

Chapter 9 Buying a New House or Apartment Versus Buying Second Hand

Buying a new house or apartment in the course of construction is significantly different from buying a secondhand property.

Here are the main differences:

1. at contract stage when buying a new property there is usually only a site which will only be a fraction of the overall value of the transaction. A secondhand property will be fully built and will have all the necessary services;

2. when buying new, the vendor is usually a limited company. A private individual or couple are the typical sellers of a secondhand house/apartment;

3. the new property will be built in accordance with a building agreement and to certain agreed standards; the legal principle of "caveat emptor" (buyer beware) applies to a second hand property;

4. there can be massive differences in the closing date of new versus second hand; second hand would be typically 4/5 weeks from the date of signing the contract.

The Contract for Sale and the Building Agreement

One of the key differences between buying new and second hand is there are 2 contracts when buying new:

1. a building agreement in respect of the house/apartment to be built and

2. a contract for the transfer of the site/agreement for transfer.

The building agreement is the most important contractual document when buying a new house/apartment. It sets out the obligations of both parties and the buyer is considered to be the "employer" and the builder the "contractor" in this agreement.

The Director of Consumer Affairs, at the urging of the Law Society, took a High Court action looking for an order to prohibit builders from using certain onerous and unfair terms and conditions. The High Court agreed to grant the order and made one which contains 15 unfair terms which are prohibited.

However, builders can, if they choose, ignore the Order and use unfair terms.

The Building Agreement

The standard Building Agreement contains a covenant by the builder to build the property to a high standard and in accordance with the plans and specifications.

The purchaser should engage the services of an architect/building surveyor/engineer to assist with ensuring that the property is built according to the plans and specifications.

The payment clause in the building agreement will provide for 10% of the purchase price of the property to be paid on signing the contract. It used to provide for stage payments being payable at different stages of the build. These payments would only be allowed by the lender on production of an interim stage payment certificate by an architect/engineer confirming that the particular stage of building has been carried out.

Generally, there were 3 stages:

1. At wall plate level

2. At roof level and

3. At the internal plastering stage.

However, in 2007 the use of stage payments was done away with through agreement between the Government and construction industry representatives.

They can still apply though to one off houses since 2007.

GENERAL CONDITIONS OF THE BUILDING AGREEMENT FOR A NEW HOUSE

The general conditions of the building agreement cover

- Possession of the site clear and fit for human habitation

- The materials to be used

- Planning permissions and building regulations

- Interest penalties being imposed for not closing on time
- Insolvency of the contractor
- Price variation
- Insurance
- Liability for defects
- Limitations on the builder's liability
- The common law rights of the purchaser
- The estate services
- The completion date
- Provision for arbitration in the event of dispute.

THE CONTRACT FOR SALE

The Contract for Sale (or Agreement for Transfer or Conveyance) will be the standard Law Society contract and provides for the transfer of the site on which the new house is built.

The most important thing to note is that it deals with the legal title to the site and the physical location, boundaries, and dimensions of the site.

The main parts of the contract will therefore contain:

- The parties

- The closing date

- Purchase price (normally a fraction of the overall cost, often 25%)

- The particulars and tenure of the property

- Special conditions

- General conditions of the standard Law Society contract.

Other critically important documents which will be required include:

1. A booklet of title showing the vendor's title

2. Replies to objections and requisitions on title

3. A section 72 declaration which will deal with deaths/voluntary dispositions on title within the last 12 years and with burdens which affect registered land, whether registered or not

4. A declaration of identity confirming that the site and all easements and services are within the boundaries of the vendor's folio/title

5. An indemnity in respect of roads and services which provides that pending the taking in charge of the estate by the Council that the developer/builder will give an indemnity to maintain them; also that there is a right to reach the public highway from the property

6. An indemnity in respect of footpaths, grass margins, and kerbs

7. The deed of assurance of the site or a lease in the case of an apartment.

CONCLUSION

As you can see, buying a new house or apartment is significantly different from buying a second hand property.

The building agreement is the biggest single difference and will almost certainly require your architect/engineer to certify that the property has been built in accordance with planning and building regulations and according to the plans and specifications.

Chapter 10 Buying in Ireland from Abroad

Thinking about buying property in Ireland? You are living outside Ireland? Or you are not an Irish citizen?

Firstly, the good news is that there are no restrictions on non Irish citizens buying property in Ireland; and this applies whether you are an EU national or a non-EU national.

The bad news, however, is that ownership of property does not entitle you to reside in Ireland. The whole area of visas, residency, immigration, work permits, asylum is a complex one and you will find more information about these topics on the Irish Naturalisation and Immigration Service website.

If you intend letting the property, and there is a very healthy residential letting market in Ireland in 2020, the tenant is obliged to withhold 20% of the annual rent and pay it over to the Irish tax authorities, the Revenue Commissioners, unless you have appointed a collection agent. The collection agent-someone like an accountant, solicitor, or estate agent-will be liable for making the tax returns on the rental income but you will have been obliged to register with the Revenue Commissioners for tax purposes prior to purchase anyway.

Property taxes

On purchasing a residential or commercial property in Ireland you will have to pay stamp duty. This is currently 1% on residential properties and 6% on commercial properties and for your solicitor to do your stamp duty return he will need a PPS or tax number for you. If you are non resident and have never had a PPS or tax number you will need to apply for one from the Department of Social Protection. You can learn more about applying for a PPS number here.

Once you buy your property you will have Local Property Tax (LPT) to pay; the amount will depend on the value of the property. You can learn more about local property tax here.

If you buy a commercial property you pay commercial rates to the local authority instead of LPT.

Buying a property in Ireland-some practical steps

One of the first things you will need to consider is instructing a solicitor to act on your behalf. Your solicitor will be able to explain how the conveyancing process works in Ireland, the various steps in a conveyance, the legal difference between a booking deposit and contract deposit, and the legal costs and outlays you will encounter.

You will also be advised to engage the services of a structural surveyor to check the structural integrity of the property, check for signs of pyrite, and check the boundaries on the ground as compared to the Property Registration Authority folio map/filed plan.

You should be aware, too, of the differences between buying a house as opposed to an apartment; the most important one will be that a management company will need to be in place to manage the common areas in a multi unit development such as an apartment development.

Property purchase costs and outlays

When budgeting for your purchase you need to account for:

- Professional legal fee
- Value added tax on the legal fee
- Property registration authority registration fees
- Structural survey
- Legal searches to be carried out on closing day to ensure there are no judgments or other unexpected burdens registered on the folio
- Commissioner for Oaths fees
- Stamp duty on purchase price

Conclusion

There is no difficulty buying property in Ireland but you will need to obtain a PPS/tax number from the Revenue Commissioners and engage the services of a solicitor early in your search.

Make sure you are dealing with a registered auctioneer/estate agent and that he/she is registered with one of the accredited auctioneering bodies in Ireland and he/she is registered with the Property Services Regulatory Authority.

Chapter 11 Bonus Chapter- Selling Your House

When selling your house your solicitor will take up your title deeds from the lending institution on accountable trust receipt (ATR). This means that your solicitor will give an undertaking to hold your deeds in trust for the bank and then discharge your mortgage once the sale has closed-this is called vacating the mortgage.

It is vital therefore that your solicitor checks with the bank that the sale proceeds will be sufficient to discharge all indebtedness secured against the property, not just the home loan.

Your solicitor, when drafting the contract for sale, will insert a special condition that the property is subject to a charge (mortgage) and this will be discharged on closing. Once he receives the sales proceeds, he will pay off the mortgage and pay the balance over to the seller, after agreed deductions (if any).

CHECKLIST FOR VENDORS OF RESIDENTIAL PROPERTY

When selling a residential property your solicitor will need certain information from you to ensure a smooth, efficient, timely transaction.

Below you will find a checklist of information that will be required:

1. Boundaries

Which are shared and which are in common with other properties?

Are there any special agreements re boundaries?

All maps and identity of the property to be checked

2. *Services*-what is the position re

Drainage?

Water?

Electricity?

Telephone?

Gas?

Alarm code?

3. Services

In charge?

Private-details/indemnity?

4. Easements

Right of way/light?

Services?

Others?

5. Forestry/fishing/sporting rights?

6. Tenancies/vacant possession to be handed over?

7. Outgoings

Ground rent?

Rates?

Water charges?

Service charge?

Insurance contribution?

Receipts and vouchers will be needed

Non principal private residence certificate of exemption or discharge will be required

LPT receipts and Revenue Commissioner's printout showing nil balance will be required

8. Notices

Served?

Given?

Compulsorily purchase order?

9. Encumbrances/Mortgage?

Mortgage of vendor?

Litigation/disputes?

Grants repayable?

10. Any Voluntary Dispositions?

11. Taxation

Capital acquisitions tax certificate of discharge?

Probate tax certificate of discharge?

Capital gains tax clearance certificate?

VAT applicable? Not normally on second hand residential properties

PPS numbers?

12. Body Corporate/Trustee

Memo and articles of association

Companies office search

Rules

Trust instrument

13. Family Law

All relevant State family law certificates?

Is the property anybody else's family home?

Any other information re family law proceedings/separation etc.

14. Planning/Building bye-laws/building regulations/fire certificate/fire services act/environmental issues?

15. Landlord/tenant

Consent to assign

Consent to change of use

16. Fee Simple Acquired?

17. Contents?

What's included?

18. Insurance?

Increase to full replacement value if necessary.

TAXES

Two taxes you will need to ensure you have paid are

1. Local property tax, including household charge from 2012
2. NPPR tax (non principal private residence)

You will need to give your solicitor proof of having a clear bill of health in relation to LPT. This is easy to do as you just need to log into the LPT website, go to your own payment history, and print out a screenshot showing a nil balance from 2012 to the date of sale.

On closing the sale, the LPT for the year of sale will be apportioned between the vendor and purchaser. This is a standard special condition of the contract of sale.

NPPR (non principal private residence) tax was introduced for second homes, for example holiday properties and/or investment properties. The tax is payable to the local authority and they will issue a Certificate of Discharge for the relevant years if you have paid it; if you are not liable because the property is your principal private residence they will issue a Certificate of Exemption for the relevant years.

In order to get this Certificate of Exemption you will need to swear a statutory declaration that the house was your principal private residence for the relevant years and send it in to your local authority.

Presenting Your House to Sell

Selling your house, and achieving the best price you can, needs to be carried out with a great degree of clinical professionalism. I know that you have a huge personal, emotional investment in the property but once you decide to sell you need to put emotion aside.

Kerb appeal

Create some kerb appeal by giving the exterior of your property a facelift. If you have a front garden, get some shrubs planted and landscaping carried out before you put the property on the market, so that there will be a bit of growth on show for viewings.

Ensure that there are no weeds around the place, sweep your footpath, mow the lawn, clean up any litter, and don't leave dirty bins sitting around. You want the 1st impression of your property to be an inviting one.

The next thing to check is your front door-could it do with a fresh coat of paint or does it need new door furniture? Ensure your porch is scrubbed clean and, if necessary, consider investing in a flower box or hanging basket to ensure a warm welcome for your viewers.

Finally, clean your windows internally and externally until they gleam; and getting in a professional window cleaner to carry out this task won't cost a fortune but will leave a lasting, positive first impression of your property.

The next step is to clean everything in your house with the motto that "if it doesn't move, clean it". And do consider getting in a professional cleaning company if this is a job that is going to prove too difficult or time consuming for you.

Start at the top of the house and work down, cleaning each room from top to bottom. Wipe furniture, shelving, door frames, and window ledges with a damp cloth, and vacuum upholstered furniture.

Polish door handles, light fittings, mirrors, pictures; use a damp cloth to clean inside cupboards, wardrobes, cabinets; check all your light fittings are working and make sure your bathroom is spotlessly clean, and don't forget to polish mirrors and taps.

In your kitchen, ensure that your cooker, fridge, washing machine, and any other appliances are sparkling. Dust your radiators and skirting boards, and vacuum all rugs, carpets, and flooring.

And don't forget the stairs!

SELL THE LIFESTYLE

It's hard to believe but, in many instances, you are not just selling your property, but a particular lifestyle. But you could get carried away spending money decorating where you run the risk of putting off your viewers with your personal style, and buying furniture just for viewings.

However, if you have a small box room or a small bedroom and they are big enough to accommodate a bed, it is a good idea to put one in to demonstrate this, even if you have to buy one.

Don't tell them-show them!

Use mirrors strategically in presenting your property; for example, if you put a mirror in a narrow room will create a sense of depth, and in a small room will create a sense of space.

Leave your bedrooms as clean and simple as possible-I know this is difficult if you have kids and are still living in the house-with fresh bed linen.

Make your living room as inviting as possible, and, if you need to, invest in a simple blind that will block an unattractive view outside.

The whole effect should be a clutter free house which promises a huge degree of calm and rest for its new owners.

Just make sure that your property is spotlessly clean, which it should be if you carry out a comprehensive cleaning job as advised already.

One Final Thing

Amazon Review

If you enjoyed this book, I would really appreciate it if you left a review on Amazon.com. This gives me great encouragement and helps others who might be helped by the information in my books.

Thanks.

Terry Gorry, August 2020

Terry Gorry & Co. Solicitors, Enfield, Co. Meath

Questions?

If you have any questions, send me an email through the contact form on my website.

Resources

If you are looking for further information about property or the law in Ireland visit my website **BusinessAndLegal.ie**. It has a great deal of free information about property and all aspects of Irish law.

Another free resource that I would recommend you check out is **my YouTube channel**. There is an entire playlist of property related videos which deal with all aspects of buying and selling property in Ireland.

Good luck with your quest for the right property for you.

About the Author

Terry Gorry is a solicitor and small business owner. He has built and run a wide range of businesses in Ireland since 1986.

Learn more about his services at any of his websites:

http://BusinessAndLegal.ie

http://EmploymentRightsIreland.com

http://SmallBusinessLawIreland.com

OTHER BOOKS BY TERRY GORRY

Employment Law in Ireland-A Guide in Plain English for Employers and Employees

27 Irish Employment Law Cases: Priceless Lessons for Employers and Employees from Decided Cases of the EAT, Equality Tribunal, and High Court

Thank You, and One Last Thing

Thank you for purchasing this book. I really appreciate it. To help me write books that help you and people like you, I would welcome any feedback you have.

Where, and how, can the book be improved?

What other topics would you like to read about?

Amazon Review

If you enjoyed this book, I would really appreciate it if you left a review on Amazon.com.

Thanks a lot and good luck with your house hunting.

Terry Gorry, 1st August 2020

Terry Gorry & Co. Solicitors

Printed in Great Britain
by Amazon